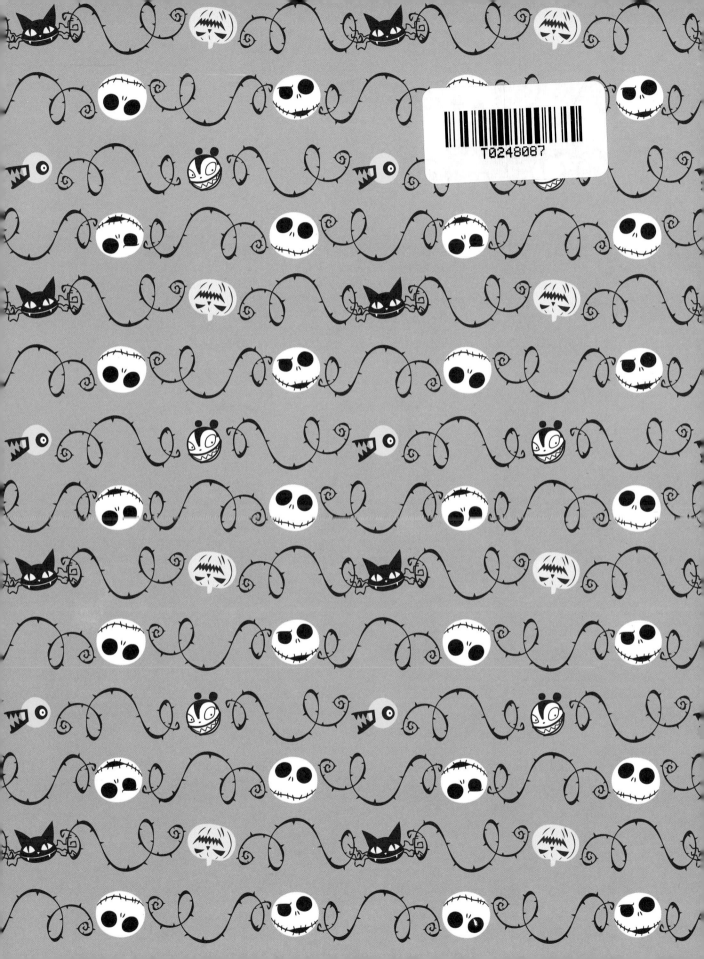

Disney

Tim Burton's
THE NIGHTMARE BEFORE CHRISTMAS

Disney

Tim Burton's THE NIGHTMARE BEFORE CHRISTMAS

THE OFFICIAL BAKING COOKBOOK

By Sandy K. Snugly

INSIGHT EDITIONS

SAN RAFAEL • LOS ANGELES • LONDON

Contents

Chapter 4:
Shuddersome Sheet Cakes

Chapter 5:
Showstopping
Spectacle Cakes

Introduction

Get ready to bake it up in eerie, cool style with *Disney Tim Burton's The Nightmare Before Christmas: The Official Baking Cookbook*, where Halloween Town comes crashing into Christmas Town, with all the fun and creepy characters and memories from the film we've come to know and love.

Even if you've watched the movie a hundred times, there's always something new to glean, some creature you didn't quite notice before, or a tiny, brilliant detail newly uncovered. *The Nightmare Before Christmas: The Official Baking Cookbook* will bring macabre joy as you flip through the pages—from simple, creepy bakes like Cyclops Eyeball Cupcakes (page 15) to frightfully delicious cookies like Cockroach Citrus Madeleines (page 63) to showstopping literal head-turners such as the Two-Faced Mayor Red Velvet Cake (page 115) or the campy Pink Easter Bunny Cut-Up Cake (page 99), the bakes in this book will have your friends and family screaming for more.

As a cake designer and artist with a specialty in character and *kawaii*-style cakes, I've always dreamt of turning the characters and scenes from *The Nightmare Before Christmas* into eerie, edible delights. The film is overflowing with a perfect mixture of gruesome and comedic details that Tim Burton fans know and love—from beloved characters such as Jack Skellington, Zero the dog, and Sandy Claws, to more obscure offerings such as The One Hiding Under Your Bed and the slithery Christmas-gift-gobbling snake. Whether you're baking ghoulish treats for your friends and family or planning an epic Halloween party or a perfectly gothic Christmas bash, let this baking cookbook lead the way to creating a deliciously macabre, eye-popping, and colorful table spread!

Tricks and Treats: Tools and Advice

The recipes in this book are marked with skill levels from Easy to Moderate to Advanced—so feel free to roll up your sleeves and choose your own baking-skill adventure!

Whenever you're starting a baking project, always make sure to read the recipe and instructions from start to finish. This way you'll ensure that you have the correct ingredients, cake pans, decorations, and special tools to complete the project.

Many recipes in this book use typical baking supplies such as muffin or cupcake tins, round cake pans, and pie pans. Other projects might call for the use of piping bags and piping tips, gel food coloring, or a specialized cake pan or cookie cutter. Even though I am a cake designer and baker by trade, I sometimes find myself without the exact tools or cookie cutter I'm looking for. Before purchasing any baking supplies, I often ask neighbors, friends, or family if they might have such a cake pan or tool to borrow. Or I'll look online for used items on sale through local online groups or social media pages—I've found many great things this way! You can also think outside the box and use creative problem-solving when it comes to decorating. For instance, licorice; fruit roll-ups; candies of all colors, shapes, sizes, and textures; and fresh fruit, herbs, and edible flowers can be used to create faces and decor of all kinds.

If you're an avid and interested baker, it couldn't hurt to invest in some fun decorating tools such as a cake turntable for frosting cakes, a simple cake decorating kit with piping bags and a few different piping tips, and a small offset spatula for applying buttercream frosting.

BUTTERCREAM TRICKS

When making buttercreams that call for icing sugar, place a damp towel over the bowl of your stand mixer and pulse to combine to avoid an icing sugar storm. Then, once incorporated, beat on high speed until doubled in volume. When coloring your buttercream, use gel color, widely available online and at baking and craft superstores. Less is more with gel color—start with a small amount before adding more color.

CAKE-FROSTING TIPS

When frosting a cake, to get a smooth finish, you will frost two layers—the first layer is called the "crumb coat," which basically traps any cake-crumb bits. Then chill the cake, and frost a second, smooth layer on top. For the crumb coat, start by frosting the entire exterior of the cake using a small offset spatula. Use a cake scraper to smooth the cake sides and place in the fridge or freezer for 15 minutes to firm up the buttercream. Add a second layer of buttercream, smoothing with the cake scraper. Now you have a smooth finish with which to further decorate!

CAKE TRICKS

Always grease and flour your cake pans before adding batter. I like to spritz my cake pans with nonstick cooking spray, or rub with butter. I also highly recommend using parchment paper cut to size to fit the bottoms of cake pans, in addition to greasing and flouring! These simple preparation tricks will prevent a lot of cakes from getting stubbornly stuck to pans. Cool your cakes in their pans on wire racks. Make sure they are completely cool before you begin frosting. You can power-chill your cakes in the fridge or freezer to get them to cool faster, if need be!

CANDY-MAKING TIPS

A few recipes call for making your own toffee or candy using a candy thermometer. Candy making features fun terms like "soft crack" and "hard crack"—terms referring to the temperature of the candy—and owning a candy thermometer has lots of fun uses, especially around the holidays.

COOKIE TRICKS

I always use parchment paper for baking cookies (or you can use reusable silicone baking mats). This way, my cookies never stick to the pan! For sugar cookies, a great tip to help your cut-out cookies maintain and hold their shape is to freeze your cut-out cookie shapes in the freezer for 15 minutes before baking. As with cakes, wait until your baked cookies are cooled before attempting to frost and decorate!

CUPCAKE TRICKS

Use paper cupcake liners for ease of baking (they can also be composted!). When dividing cupcake batter, fill each cupcake liner ⅔ full with batter. I use a large retractable ice cream scoop to dole out my cupcake batter in even portions! If you do a lot of cupcake, muffin, and cookie baking, retractable ice cream scoops are awesome to help achieve even amounts of batters and cookie doughs.

EDIBLE FLOWER TIPS

Choose organic edible flowers that you've purchased at the farmers' market, grown yourself in little pots, or found in the herbs section at some grocery stores.

FONDANT TIPS

Fondant is fun when it comes to cake decorating, especially when making facial features for all the lovable characters from *The Nightmare Before Christmas*! To work with fondant, make sure your hands are clean and dry. Fondant adheres to itself with tiny amounts of water: It becomes sticky and tacky and dries like glue. For creating various shapes (such as eyes or tentacles!) using fondant, you can either mold shapes using your hands or cut out fondant shapes using small circular cookie cutters or the bottom round edge of piping tips in various sizes. A sharp paring knife can be used for cutting out fondant shapes. Prepurchased fondant comes in many colors, but when coloring fondant with gel food coloring, use very little gel coloring, wear food-safe gloves, and use a little bit of cornstarch to mix in, in case things get sticky.

LEVELING CAKE TRICKS

Sometimes cake layers might bake up with a slight dome. Leveling your cake will give you an even, flat layer which is easier for stacking your cakes when making some of the layered cake projects. Make sure your cake is cooled; use a sharp serrated bread knife and use a gentle sawing action to trim your cakes. You can also level sheet cakes in the same way. Cake scraps can be used to make parfaits or serve with ice cream for a yummy snack!

PIE DOUGH TIPS

When preparing a butter pie dough, for the flakiest results, here's a Dr. Finkelstein tip: Do not entirely incorporate the ingredients. Instead, aim to have visible pieces of butter remaining and even a few floury bits, keeping everything cold by not overhandling the dough.

PIPING BAG TIPS

Plastic or reusable piping bags and tips are available widely online and at baking and craft superstores. I reuse my plastic piping bags by washing them with hot soapy water, rinsing, and drying. Snip off the pointy end of the piping bag (don't snip too much— you just want your piping bag to nestle in to the tip) and insert the piping tip. Place your piping bag in a large glass and fold the sides over the glass. Fill your piping bag half-full with buttercream, twist the bag closed, and it's ready to use!

PIPING TIP TIPS

Piping tips are the metal nozzles used in conjunction with piping bags to create special buttercream shapes, allowing us to have fun with buttercream piping and decorating. The most common piping tips used in this book are open star tips, multipronged open star tips, open circle tips, and multi-opening tips (also known as the grass tip—I use this one to mimic hair in a few instances).

ROYAL ICING TRICKS

Royal icing is fantastic for creating smooth and artistic cookies. Note that royal icing can dry out very quickly. Always cover your bowls of royal icing with a damp towel. Royal icing can also be thickened and thinned easily. To thicken royal icing, add increments of powdered sugar (also referred to as confectioners' or icing sugar), 1 teaspoon at a time. To thin out royal icing, add very small increments of water, ⅛ teaspoon at a time, until desired consistency. Slightly thicker icing is perfect for outlining your cookies, such as Sally Blue Helping Hands Cookies (page 69), and thinner icing is perfect for "flooding" your cookies with colored icing. Let the icing completely dry overnight before adding the next layer of decoration (such as Sally's nail polish and stitches).

VANILLA BEAN TIPS

To remove the vanilla bean seeds from the pod, use a sharp paring knife to slit the bean open. Use the knife to scrape the seeds from the pod. You can use the leftover pod to flavor a jar of granulated sugar, turning it into vanilla sugar. Vanilla bean paste is a great alternative to a whole vanilla bean, and not as expensive. Look for vanilla bean paste online, at specialty food shops, and in some grocery stores.

— **Chapter 1** —

Creepy Cupcakes and Blood-Curdling Bakes

Cyclops Eyeball Cupcakes

These creepy spect-*ocular* cupcakes will have your party goers begging for more as they bite into the tantalizing coconut grape jelly treats. The eyeballs are made with coconut milk and agar-agar, also known as nature's gelatin, for a firm set. The eyeballs then peek out of a piped grape jelly buttercream swirl! These cupcakes demand to be seen.

Yield: 24 cupcakes | Skill Level: Easy

FOR THE COCONUT CUPCAKES

2½ cups cake flour
½ cup shredded white coconut
1 teaspoon baking powder
1 teaspoon fine sea salt
1 cup unsalted butter, room temperature
2 cups granulated sugar
2 eggs
1 teaspoon pure vanilla extract or toasted coconut extract
1¼ cups full-fat coconut milk

FOR THE GRAPE JELLY BUTTERCREAM

2 cups unsalted butter, room temperature
3½ cups icing sugar, sifted
½ cup Concord grape jelly
⅛ teaspoon fine sea salt

FOR THE COCONUT JELLY EYEBALLS

One 13.5-ounce can full-fat coconut milk
¼ cup granulated sugar
1 tablespoon agar-agar powder
Blue gel food coloring

DECORATING INGREDIENTS AND TOOLS

2 cupcake pans
Cupcake liners
Food-grade 10-gauge syringe
One silicone 1½-inch to 2-inch semi-sphere ball mold
Piping bag fitted with an open star tip

TO MAKE THE CUPCAKES: Preheat the oven to 350°F. Line two cupcake pans with cupcake liners in your choice of color and set aside.

In a large bowl, whisk together the cake flour, shredded coconut, baking powder, and salt to combine and set aside.

In the bowl of a stand mixer fitted with the paddle attachment or in a large bowl with a handheld mixer, beat the butter and sugar on high speed until doubled in volume, about 1 minute. Scrape down the sides of the bowl with a spatula as needed.

With the mixer on low speed, add the eggs, one at a time, until incorporated. Add the vanilla extract or toasted coconut extract and mix until combined.

With the mixer on low speed, alternate between adding the flour mixture in three equal portions and the coconut milk in two equal portions, beginning and ending with the flour mixture, mixing in total for 1 to 2 minutes, until a smooth batter forms.

Divide the batter evenly into the prepared cupcake pans, filling each cavity no more than ⅔ full. Bake for 20 to 24 minutes, until a cake tester inserted into the center of the cupcake comes out with only moist crumbs. Let cool completely on wire racks.

TO MAKE THE BUTTERCREAM: In the bowl of a stand mixer fitted with a paddle attachment or in a large bowl with a hand mixer, beat the butter, icing sugar, Concord grape jelly, and salt on high speed until doubled in volume, 1 to 2 minutes.

TO MAKE THE COCONUT JELLY EYEBALLS: In a medium saucepan set over medium heat, whisk together the coconut milk, sugar, and agar-agar. Bring to a gentle boil, and keep gently whisking until sugar and agar-agar powder have completely dissolved, 1 to 2 minutes. Divide the coconut jelly, placing ½ cup into a small bowl. Tint the ½ cup of jelly using the blue gel coloring. Using the food-grade syringe, place a small blob of blue coconut jelly into the center of each cavity of the semi-sphere ball mold. Let it set in the fridge for 10 minutes. Wash out the food-grade syringe. Remove the mold from the fridge and, using the food grade syringe, suck up the white coconut jelly and carefully fill the rest of each cavity with the jelly. Place in refrigerator to set overnight. Note: If the jelly sets before you fill the mold, simply reheat on low heat to liquefy.

TO DECORATE THE CUPCAKES: Unmold the white coconut eyeballs. Fill the piping bag fitted with the open star tip with the grape jelly buttercream. Holding the piping bag at a 90-degree angle, start at the outer edge of the cupcake and squeeze the piping bag. Continue squeezing as you pipe a circle, working your way inward, piping two rotations. Pull upward to finish. Place a jelly eyeball in the center of each cupcake and enjoy!

Deadly Nightshade Blue Cake Parfaits

Elegant and beautifully blue—the deadly nightshade is coming for you! If Sally were to make Dr. Finkelstein a perniciously sweet treat in an attempt to escape her tower, she would surely serve up these blue vanilla bean cake parfaits in champagne flutes or parfait cups! If you don't have either of those, little jam jars will do. Decorate with fresh blueberries and edible bachelor's button flowers to keep your guests wondering if they'll make it through the night! For the toffee crunch, you can either make your own (recipe included here!) or purchase toffee bits, which are often found in the same grocery aisle as chocolate chips.

Yield: 12 cake parfaits | Skill Level: Easy

FOR THE VANILLA SPONGE CAKE
5 large egg whites
½ teaspoon cream of tartar
⅛ teaspoon fine sea salt
10 tablespoons granulated sugar, divided
5 large egg yolks
1 teaspoon vanilla bean paste or pure vanilla extract
2 tablespoons unsalted butter, melted
¼ cup heavy cream
½ cup cake flour

FOR THE BLUE VANILLA BEAN BUTTERCREAM
1½ cups unsalted butter, room temperature
2 cups icing sugar, sifted
2 teaspoons vanilla bean paste or pure vanilla extract
⅛ teaspoon fine sea salt
⅛ teaspoon blue gel food coloring

FOR THE TOFFEE BITS
½ cup unsalted butter
1 cup light brown sugar
1 teaspoon fine sea salt

DECORATING INGREDIENTS AND TOOLS
10-by-15-inch baking pan (or two 8-inch round cake pans)
Offset spatula
Rimmed baking sheet (if making toffee)
Candy thermometer (if making toffee)
Piping bag fitted with an open star tip
12 parfait cups or glass jam jars
Circle-shaped cookie cutter (optional)
Fresh blueberries
Edible bachelor's button flowers (or other edible flowers)

TO MAKE THE CAKE: Preheat the oven to 375°F. Grease the baking pan with vegetable oil or nonstick spray and cut a piece of parchment paper to size.

In the bowl of a stand mixer fitted with the whisk attachment or a large bowl with a hand mixer, beat the egg whites, cream of tartar, and salt on high speed until frothy, about 1 minute. With the mixer on, slowly add 5 tablespoons sugar, 1 teaspoon at a time, until you've created a meringue with stiff peaks, about 2 minutes.

In a medium bowl, whisk the egg yolks and remaining 5 tablespoons sugar until light and pale yellow in color, about 2 minutes. Add the vanilla bean paste, melted butter, and heavy cream and whisk until incorporated.

Sift the cake flour into the egg yolk mixture, using a rubber spatula to fold until incorporated.

Gently fold the meringue mixture into the egg yolk mixture in three batches, being careful to not deflate the meringue too much.

Pour the cake batter into the prepared cake pan, using an offset spatula to carefully spread the batter to the edges. Bake for 10 to 12 minutes, until a toothpick inserted into the center comes out with only moist crumbs. Place on a wire rack to cool completely.

CONTINUES ON PAGE 18

TO MAKE THE BUTTERCREAM: In the bowl of a stand mixer fitted with a paddle attachment or a large bowl with a hand mixer, beat the butter, icing sugar, vanilla bean paste, salt, and blue gel food coloring on high speed until doubled in volume, 1 to 2 minutes.

TO MAKE THE TOFFEE CRUNCH: Prepare a rimmed baking sheet with parchment paper or a reusable silicone baking mat.

In a small, heavy-bottomed saucepan, melt the butter over medium heat. Add the sugar and salt, whisking vigorously to combine, about 1 minute. Cook, stirring constantly, until the candy is thickened and golden and your candy thermometer reaches 290°F to 300°F (low end of the hard-crack stage).

Carefully pour the hot candy mixture onto the prepared baking sheet. Let cool and harden completely. Use a rolling pin to whack the candy into toffee bits. You can make some larger shards for artful decoration of your parfaits!

TO ASSEMBLE THE PARFAITS: Fill your piping bag with the blue buttercream. Pipe a layer of buttercream on the bottom of your parfait cup or jam jar. (You can also just spoon it in, but it's a cleaner method using the piping bag!). Using a circle cookie cutter, punch out pieces of the cooled vanilla cake. Place a piece of cake on top of the buttercream, pressing down. Add another layer of buttercream and a generous sprinkle of toffee bits. Continue layering until you reach the top of the parfait; finish with a buttercream swirl, dotted with fresh blueberries, toffee shards, and edible flowers, if using!

Piped Jack-o'-Lantern Cupcakes

Pump up the party with these simple Halloween Town jack-o'-lantern-inspired cupcakes, piped using a large open circle tip, then dipped into a bowl of orange sanding sugar. Decorate with a little chocolate or pretzel-stick stem, and use easy chocolate ganache (or chocolate pieces) to pipe on a face. Arrange on a platter for your own little scrumptiously edible pumpkin patch—keep them cute or make them creepy enough to delight any resident of Halloween Town!

Yield: 24 cupcakes | Skill Level: Easy

FOR THE CUPCAKES

2 cups all-purpose flour

1 teaspoon baking soda

1 teaspoon baking powder

1 teaspoon fine sea salt

1 teaspoon ground cinnamon

1 teaspoon ground ginger

1 cup unsalted butter, room temperature

1 cup packed brown sugar

½ cup granulated sugar

2 large eggs

1 teaspoon pure vanilla extract

One 15-ounce can pumpkin puree

FOR THE MAPLE BUTTERCREAM

1½ cups unsalted butter, room temperature

2 cups icing sugar, sifted

½ cup maple syrup, or 1 teaspoon pure maple extract

⅛ teaspoon fine sea salt

DECORATING INGREDIENTS AND TOOLS

2 cupcake pans

Black cupcake liners

Green gel food coloring

Piping bag fitted with a small leaf tip

Piping bag fitted with a large open circle tip

Orange sanding sugar

Chocolate bar cut into stem-like pieces and jack-o'-lantern-style pieces

TO MAKE THE CUPCAKES: Preheat the oven to 350°F. Line two cupcake pans with black cupcake liners and set aside.

In a large bowl, whisk together the flour, baking soda, baking powder, salt, cinnamon, and ginger.

In the bowl of a stand mixer fitted with the paddle attachment or in a large bowl with a handheld mixer, beat the butter with the brown sugar and granulated sugar on high speed until doubled in volume, about 1 minute. Using a spatula, scrape down the sides of the bowl as needed.

With the mixer on low speed, add the eggs one at a time, mixing until incorporated. Add the vanilla extract. Add the pumpkin puree on low speed, mixing to combine, about 30 seconds.

With the mixer on low speed, add the flour mixture and mix to combine until smooth and incorporated, about 1 minute.

Divide the batter evenly into the prepared cupcake tins, filling each cavity no more than ⅔ full. Bake for 20 to 24 minutes, until a cake tester inserted into the center of a cupcake comes out with only moist crumbs. Let cool completely on wire racks.

TO MAKE THE BUTTERCREAM: In the bowl of a stand mixer fitted with a paddle attachment or in a large bowl with a handheld mixer, beat the butter, icing sugar, maple syrup, and salt on high speed until doubled in volume, 1 to 2 minutes.

TO DECORATE THE CUPCAKES: In a small bowl, place ¼ cup of the buttercream. Add a toothpick tip's amount of green gel food coloring, mixing to combine. Add this green buttercream to the piping bag fitted with the leaf tip.

Fill the piping bag fitted with a large open circle tip with the uncolored buttercream and set aside. Fill a small bowl with the orange sanding sugar.

Holding the piping bag with the circle tip at a 90-degree angle on top of a cupcake, squeeze the piping bag to create a large dollop of buttercream, to fill the whole cupcake. Place the dollop into the sanding sugar, gently pressing the sugar to the buttercream as you shape it into a ball-like pumpkin shape. Place the cupcake right side up and decorate with chocolate stem and chocolate face pieces. Using the piping bag with the leaf tip, pipe little leaves around the chocolate stem. Repeat with the remaining cupcakes!

Christmas Tree Gingerbread Cupcakes

When Jack Skellington enters Christmas Town, he is dazzled by the sights of an entirely new holiday—shimmering Christmas lights strung up all over town, piles of fluffy snow, and Christmas trees galore! These cozy gingerbread cupcakes are topped with ice cream sugar cones, piped to look just like the Christmas trees Jack sees! Add Halloween-themed sprinkles to the Christmas trees to give them a Halloween Town touch.

Yield: 24 cupcakes | Skill Level: Easy

FOR THE GINGERBREAD CUPCAKES

3 cups all-purpose flour
1 tablespoon ground ginger
2 teaspoons ground cinnamon
1 teaspoon baking soda
1 teaspoon fine sea salt
1 cup unsalted butter, room temperature
1 cup light brown sugar, packed
1 cup granulated sugar
1 cup molasses
4 large eggs, room temperature
1 tablespoon pure vanilla extract
1 cup buttermilk

FOR LEMON CREAM CHEESE FROSTING

1 cup cream cheese, room temperature
1 cup unsalted butter, room temperature
4 cups icing sugar, sifted
Pinch of salt
Zest of one lemon

FOR THE GREEN VANILLA BUTTERCREAM

1½ cups unsalted butter, room temperature
3 cups icing sugar, sifted
2 teaspoons pure vanilla extract
½ teaspoon green gel food coloring
Pinch of salt

DECORATING INGREDIENTS AND TOOLS

2 cupcake pans
Cupcake liners
Piping bag fitted with a large open circle tip
24 ice cream sugar cones
Small offset spatula
Piping bag fitted with a leaf tip
Candies and sprinkles
Icing sugar, for dusting

TO MAKE THE CUPCAKES: Preheat the oven to 350°F. Line two cupcake pans with cupcake liners in your choice of color and set aside.

In a large bowl, whisk together the flour, ginger, cinnamon, baking soda, and salt and set aside.

In the bowl of a stand mixer fitted with the paddle attachment or in a large bowl with a handheld mixer, beat together the butter, brown sugar, granulated sugar, and molasses on high speed until light and fluffy, about 2 minutes, scraping down the sides of the bowl as needed.

With the mixer on low speed, add the eggs one at a time until incorporated. Add the vanilla and mix until incorporated.

With the mixer on low speed, alternate between adding the dry ingredients and the buttermilk in three equal portions, beginning and ending with the dry ingredients, until a smooth batter forms, about 1 minute total.

Divide the batter evenly into prepared cupcake pans, filling each cavity no more than ⅔ full. Bake for 20 to 24 minutes, until a cake tester inserted into the center of the cupcake comes out with only moist crumbs. Let cool completely on wire racks.

CONTINUES ON PAGE 22

TO MAKE THE LEMON CREAM CHEESE FROSTING: In the bowl of a stand mixer fitted with the paddle attachment or a large bowl with a handheld mixer, beat the cream cheese, butter, icing sugar, salt, and lemon zest on medium speed until incorporated.

TO MAKE THE GREEN VANILLA BUTTERCREAM: In the bowl of a stand mixer fitted with the paddle attachment or a large bowl with a handheld mixer, beat the butter, icing sugar, vanilla extract, green gel food coloring, and salt on high speed until doubled in volume, about 2 minutes.

TO ASSEMBLE THE CUPCAKES: Fill the piping bag fitted with the large open circle tip with the lemon cream cheese frosting. Pipe one dollop of frosting on the top of each cupcake.

Working with one cupcake at a time, place a sugar cone on top of the cupcake frosting dollop, pressing down to nestle the cone into the frosting. Use the small offset spatula to frost a thin coating of green vanilla buttercream to the cone. Repeat for all the cupcakes.

Fill the piping bag fitted with the leaf tip with the remaining green vanilla buttercream. Starting from the bottom of the cone, pipe leaves all the way up and around the cone to resemble a spiky pine tree. You can also use an open star or multipronged star tip to make the tree.

Decorate each tree with Halloween-themed sprinkles, if desired, or with small candies to resemble Christmas baubles. Dust the entire tree with icing sugar to finish.

White Spider Jam Cupcakes

Jack Skellington attempts to understand what Christmas is all about by experimenting in his science lab of tricks and treats, cutting out what he thinks will be a holiday snowflake but in fact turns out to be a spider! Skittering spiders are welcome friends in Halloween Town—and these piped white buttercream spider cupcakes inspired by Jack's spider snowflakes will be extra welcome on your holiday dessert table!

Yield: 24 cupcakes | Skill Level: Moderate

FOR THE CHOCOLATE COCONUT CUPCAKES

2½ cups all-purpose flour

2 cups granulated sugar

1½ cups Dutch-process cocoa powder

2½ teaspoons baking soda

1¼ teaspoons baking powder

1¼ teaspoons fine sea salt

2 eggs, room temperature

2¼ cups full-fat coconut milk

½ cup plus 2 tablespoons vegetable oil

1 teaspoon pure vanilla extract

FOR THE VANILLA SWISS MERINGUE BUTTERCREAM

½ lemon

1 cup egg whites (about 8 large egg whites)

2¼ cups granulated sugar

2¼ cups unsalted butter, room temperature

2 teaspoons pure vanilla extract

Pinch of fine sea salt

DECORATING INGREDIENTS AND TOOLS

2 cupcake pans

Cupcake liners

Paring knife

Raspberry jam

Piping bag fitted with a large open circle tip

Round chocolate wafer cookies

White chocolate sprinkles

Piping bag fitted with a small open circle tip

Black decorating gel

Candy thermometer

TO MAKE THE CUPCAKES: Preheat the oven to 350°F. Line two cupcake pans with cupcake liners in your choice of color and set aside.

In the bowl of a stand mixer fitted with the paddle attachment or in a large bowl using a handheld mixer, mix together on low speed the flour, sugar, cocoa powder, baking soda, baking powder, and salt until combined.

With the mixer on low speed, add the eggs, coconut milk, vegetable oil, and vanilla extract, mixing until combined, about 1 minute.

Divide the batter evenly into prepared cupcake pans, filling each cavity no more than ⅔ full. Bake for 20 to 24 minutes, until a cake tester inserted into the center of the cupcake comes out with only moist crumbs. Let cool completely on wire racks.

TO MAKE THE MERINGUE BUTTERCREAM: Ensure that the metal bowl of your stand mixer is completely grease-free by wiping it with a halved lemon, then rinse and dry it thoroughly.

In the bowl of a stand mixer fitted with the whisk attachment or a large bowl with a handheld mixer, mix the egg whites and sugar on low speed to combine into a sugar slurry. Fill a medium saucepan with a few inches of water and place it on the stove top over medium-high heat. Set the mixer bowl on top of the saucepan to create a double boiler, making sure the mixer bowl doesn't touch the water.

Heat the egg and sugar mixture until it reaches 160°F on a thermometer, whisking occasionally, 5 to 7 minutes.

Carefully return the mixing bowl to the stand mixer with the whisk attachment in place. Bring the mixer up to high speed and beat the mixture for 8 to 10 minutes, until you've reached stiff peaks and a billowy meringue.

Swap out the whisk for the paddle attachment. Make sure your meringue has cooled sufficiently enough so that when you add the butter it won't completely melt away. The bowl should be only slightly warm at this point.

With the mixer on low speed, add the butter a few pieces at a time, until all the butter is incorporated—it will look like thick soup at this point. Add the vanilla extract and pinch of salt.

Bring the mixer speed up to medium-high and beat until a fluffy meringue buttercream forms, 2 to 3 minutes.

CONTINUES ON PAGE 25

TO ASSEMBLE THE CUPCAKES: Using a paring knife, cut a 1-inch divot from each cupcake and fill the hole with 1 tablespoon jam. from each cupcake and fill the hole with raspberry jam. Place the divot back on top.

Fill the piping bag fitted with the large open circle tip with half of the buttercream. Pipe dollops of buttercream in the center of each cupcake. Place a round chocolate wafer cookie on top of each dollop, gently pressing down to squish the buttercream to the edges.

On top of the wafer cookie, pipe a small dollop of buttercream to form the head of a spider, then a larger bulbous dollop of buttercream to form the spider's body. Sprinkle a few white chocolate sprinkles on top of the body, pressing in to adhere (to make the spider hairy!).

Fill the second piping bag fitted with the small open circle tip with the remaining buttercream. Pipe four legs on each side of the spider's body. Using the black decorating gel, pipe two eyes on the head. Pipe two fangs coming out of the spider's head. Add a toothpick tip's worth of raspberry jam to the fangs to emulate blood.

Bag of Bugs Hi-Hat Cupcakes

After Jack and Oogie Boogie battle it out in Oogie Boogie's lair, Oogie Boogie ultimately meets his seam-splitting end, revealing his bug-infested insides. Inspired by that moment, when you slice into these neon-candy-dipped chocolate-vanilla cupcakes, creepy yet delicious insect critters spill out. This is the perfect surprise-inside treat to make your party guests howl with delight.

Yield: 24 cupcakes | Skill Level: Moderate

FOR THE CHOCOLATE CUPCAKES

1 cup whole milk

1 teaspoon white vinegar

1¾ cups all-purpose flour

2 cups granulated sugar

1 cup Dutch-process cocoa powder

2 teaspoons baking soda

1 teaspoon baking powder

1 teaspoon fine sea salt

½ cup vegetable oil

2 large eggs, room temperature

2 teaspoons pure vanilla extract

¾ cup freshly brewed hot coffee

FOR THE VANILLA BUTTERCREAM

2 cups unsalted butter, room temperature

4 cups icing sugar, sifted

4 teaspoons pure vanilla extract

⅛ teaspoon fine sea salt

DECORATING INGREDIENTS AND TOOLS

2 cupcake pans

Cupcake liners

Paring knife

Piping bag fitted with a large open circle tip

Candy insects such as spiders, worms, and other bugs

Four 12-ounce packages candy melts in bright green

1 teaspoon coconut oil

Black decorating gel

Black royal icing (optional)

Chocolate ganache (optional)

TO MAKE THE CUPCAKES: Preheat the oven to 350°F. Line two cupcake pans with cupcake liners in your choice of color and set aside.

In a medium bowl, mix together the whole milk and the white vinegar. Let the mixture sit until curdled, about 10 minutes.

In the bowl of a stand mixer fitted with the paddle attachment or in a large bowl using a handheld mixer, mix together on low speed the flour, sugar, cocoa powder, baking soda, baking powder, and salt.

Once the milk is curdled, whisk it in a large bowl with the vegetable oil, eggs, and vanilla extract until combined.

With the mixer on low speed, slowly pour the milk mixture into the flour mixture. Add the hot coffee and mix until the batter is just incorporated, about 30 seconds.

Divide the batter evenly into prepared cupcake pans, filling each cavity no more than ⅔ full. Bake for 20 to 24 minutes, until a cake tester inserted into the center of the cupcake comes out with only moist crumbs. Let cool completely on wire racks.

TO MAKE THE BUTTERCREAM: In the bowl of a stand mixer fitted with a paddle attachment or in a large bowl with a handheld mixer, beat the butter, icing sugar, vanilla extract, and salt on high speed until doubled in volume, 1 to 2 minutes.

TO ASSEMBLE THE CUPCAKES: Using a paring knife, cut a large divot from the top of each cupcake. Make an Oogie Boogie–style buttercream swirl in two steps. Fill the piping bag fitted with the open circle tip with the vanilla buttercream. Pipe concentric circles of buttercream, working your way up as you stack them but leaving a hole in the center. Fill the divot and hole in the buttercream with candy bugs. Finish the buttercream swirl by piping another circle and pulling upward in the center to create Oogie Boogie's pointy head. Continue with all the cupcakes, then refrigerate for 1 hour, until the buttercream has firmed up.

For the next step, for easy cleanup, set a wire rack over a sheet of parchment paper to catch any candy melt drips. You may want to melt each candy melt package separately, in case you don't need to use all four packages.

CONTINUES ON PAGE 28

Melt the green candy melts along with the teaspoon of coconut oil according to the package instructions, stirring together to combine. Pour the candy melts into a wide-mouthed glass or bowl that's deep enough to dip Oogie Boogie's buttercream frosting head into.

Remove the chilled buttercream-piped cupcakes from the refrigerator. Dip the first cupcake's buttercream into the bright green melted candy, letting any excess drip off. Place the cupcake on the wire rack to dry completely; continue with all the cupcakes.

Once the cupcake coating is firm and dry, use the black decorating gel to paint on Oogie Boogie's signature eyes and wide mouth. Alternatively, you can use royal icing, dyed black using gel coloring, or chocolate ganache cooled to a piping consistency to pipe on the face.

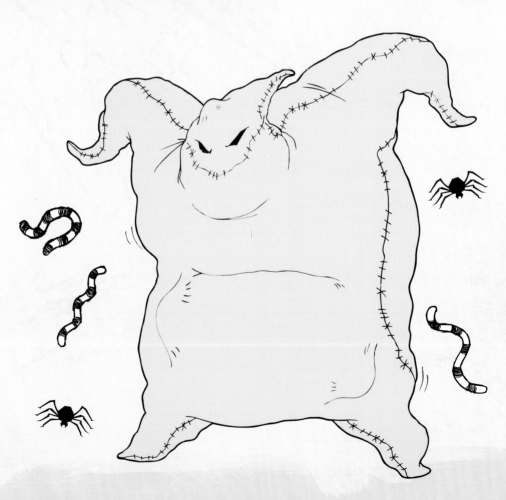

Sally Thistle Flower Earl Grey Cupcakes

Sally would surely love these buttercream-piped thistle flower cupcakes, inspired by the flowers she picks as she wonders if Jack returns her romantic feelings. Perfect for a gothic tea party, these Earl Grey tea-infused cupcakes would look petrifyingly perfect on a cake stand adorned with dried (dead!) flowers. Pluck the frosting petals (with your teeth) and maybe your skeletal romance dreams will come true.

Yield: 24 cupcakes | Skill Level: Moderate

FOR THE EARL GREY BUTTER

3 cups unsalted butter

Loose tea from 6 Earl Grey tea bags (or ⅜ cup loose-leaf Earl Grey tea)

FOR THE EARL GREY CUPCAKES

1 cup Earl Grey butter

3 cups cake flour

1 tablespoon baking powder

¾ teaspoon fine sea salt

1¾ cups granulated sugar

4 large eggs

1 teaspoon pure vanilla extract

1¼ cups whole milk

FOR THE EARL GREY BUTTERCREAM

2 cups Earl Grey butter

½ lemon

½ cup plus 2 tablespoons egg whites

1¼ cups granulated sugar

1½ teaspoons vanilla bean paste

DECORATING INGREDIENTS AND TOOLS

2 cupcake pans

Cupcake liners

Green, navy blue, and violet gel food coloring

Piping bag fitted with a leaf tip

Piping bag fitted with a medium open circle tip

Piping bag fitted with a small multipronged open-star tip

Candy thermometer

TO MAKE THE EARL GREY BUTTER: In a small saucepan, melt the butter. Add the loose Earl Grey tea leaves, remove from the heat, and let the flavor infuse the butter for 10 minutes. Using a fine mesh strainer, strain and discard the tea leaves; bits of tea will remain in the butter, which is fine; they'll add flavor. Refrigerate the tea butter and allow to firm up to room temperature, about 10 minutes.

TO MAKE THE CUPCAKES: Preheat the oven to 350°F. Line two cupcake pans with cupcake liners in your choice of color and set aside.

In a large bowl, whisk together the cake flour, baking powder, and salt and set aside.

In the bowl of a stand mixer fitted with the paddle attachment or in a large bowl using a handheld mixer, beat the tea butter and granulated sugar on high speed until light and fluffy, scraping down the sides of the bowl as needed, about 2 minutes.

With the mixer on low speed, add the eggs one at a time until incorporated. Add the vanilla extract and mix to incorporate.

With the mixer on low speed, alternate between adding the flour mixture and adding the whole milk in three equal portions, beginning and ending with the flour mixture, until a smooth batter forms, about 1 minute total.

Divide the batter evenly into the prepared cupcake pans, filling each cavity no more than ⅔ full. Bake for 20 to 24 minutes, until a cake tester inserted into the center of the cupcake comes out with only moist crumbs. Let cool completely on wire racks.

TO MAKE THE BUTTERCREAM: Ensure that the metal bowl of your stand mixer is completely grease-free by wiping it with a halved lemon, then rinse and dry it thoroughly.

In the bowl of a stand mixer fitted with the whisk attachment or a large bowl with a handheld mixer, mix the egg whites and sugar on low speed to combine into a sugar slurry. Fill a medium saucepan with a few inches of water and place it on the stove top over medium-high heat. Set the mixer bowl on top of the saucepan to create a double boiler, making sure the mixer bowl doesn't touch the water.

CONTINUES ON PAGE 31

Heat the egg and sugar mixture until it reaches 160°F on a thermometer, whisking occasionally, 5 to 7 minutes.

Carefully return the mixing bowl to the stand mixer, with the whisk attachment in place. Bring the mixer up to high speed and beat the mixture for 8 to 10 minutes, until you've reached stiff peaks and a billowy meringue and the meringue has cooled from the whipping.

Swap out the whisk for the paddle attachment. Make sure your meringue has cooled sufficiently enough so that when you add the butter it won't completely melt away. The bowl should be only slightly warm at this point.

With the mixer on low speed, add the tea butter a few pieces at a time, until all the butter is incorporated—it will look like thick soup at this point. Add the vanilla bean paste and pinch of salt.

Bring the mixer speed up to medium-high and beat until a fluffy meringue buttercream forms, 2 to 3 minutes.

TO ASSEMBLE THE CUPCAKES: Add 1 cup of the buttercream to a small bowl. Add a toothpick tip's worth of green gel food coloring and mix until combined. Add this buttercream to the piping bag fitted with the leaf tip.

Add 1 teaspoon navy blue and 1 teaspoon violet gel food coloring to the remaining buttercream, mixing to combine. Divide the buttercream and fill both the piping bag fitted with the medium open circle tip and the piping bag fitted with a small multipronged open star with the violet-blue buttercream.

Using the blue buttercream with the larger tip, pipe onto the center of a cupcake a chocolate kiss-like blob shape, with a point on top. Using the small tip, start at the bottom of the dollop and pipe little spikes all along the bottom, working your way up in circles to pipe the entire dollop with little spikes.

With the green buttercream, pipe leaves tucked into and around the bottom of the blue thistle. Repeat with the remaining cupcakes!

Shock's Witchy Hat Cupcakes

Lock, Shock, and Barrel are Oogie Boogie's helpers, and they love to stir up trouble, finding ways at every turn to cause a little chaos. These wicked cupcakes, inspired by Shock's purple pointy hat, are certain to enchant your friends and family—no tricks required!

Yield: 24 cupcakes | Skill Level: Moderate

FOR THE VANILLA CUPCAKES

3 cups all-purpose flour
1 tablespoon baking powder
1 teaspoon fine sea salt
1 cup unsalted butter
1¾ cups granulated sugar
4 eggs, room temperature
1 tablespoon pure vanilla extract
1¼ cups whole milk

FOR THE SALTED CARAMEL

1 cup granulated sugar
6 tablespoons unsalted butter, room temperature
½ cup heavy cream, room temperature
1 teaspoon fine sea salt

FOR THE SALTED CARAMEL BUTTERCREAM

2 cups unsalted butter, room temperature
3 cups icing sugar, sifted
1 teaspoon vanilla bean paste or pure vanilla extract
¼ cup salted caramel
Green gel food coloring (optional)

DECORATING INGREDIENTS AND TOOLS

2 cupcake pans
Cupcake liners
Paring knife
Piping bag fitted with a large open circle tip
Purple sanding sugar (enough for 24 cupcakes)
One 12-ounce package of purple candy melts
1 teaspoon coconut oil
12 chocolate sandwich cookies, separated and filling discarded
24 mini ice cream sugar cones
Pink fondant

TO MAKE THE CUPCAKES: Preheat the oven to 350°F. Line two cupcake pans with cupcake liners in your choice of color and set aside.

In a large bowl, whisk together the flour, baking powder, and salt and set aside.

In the bowl of a stand mixer fitted with the paddle attachment or in a large bowl using a handheld mixer, beat the butter and sugar on high speed until light and fluffy, scraping down the sides of the bowl as needed, about 2 minutes.

With the mixer on low speed, add the eggs one at a time until incorporated. Add the vanilla extract and mix to incorporate.

With the mixer on low speed, alternate between adding the flour mixture and adding the whole milk in three equal portions, beginning and ending with the flour mixture, until a smooth batter forms, about 1 minute total.

Divide the batter evenly into the prepared cupcake pans, filling each cavity no more than ⅔ full. Bake for 20 to 24 minutes, until a cake tester inserted into the center of the cupcake comes out with only moist crumbs. Let cool completely on wire racks.

TO MAKE THE SALTED CARAMEL: In a medium heavy-bottomed saucepan, heat the sugar on medium-high heat, stirring constantly with a wooden spoon. Melt the sugar until it forms an amber-colored, thickened liquid, 3 to 4 minutes.

Immediately stir in the butter until melted and combined. Note: The caramel will bubble, so be aware and wear appropriate clothing (apron, oven mitts).

Stir mixture constantly and very slowly pour in the heavy cream. Again, be careful—the mixture will bubble up. Whisk to combine and allow to boil for about 1 minute. Remove from heat, and whisk in the salt.

Cool completely before using. Caramel will thicken as it cools.

TO MAKE THE BUTTERCREAM: In the bowl of a stand mixer fitted with the paddle attachment or a large bowl with a handheld mixer, combine the butter, icing sugar, vanilla bean paste, salted caramel, and green gel food coloring, if using, on low speed. Increase to high speed and beat until buttercream is light and fluffy and doubled in volume, 1 to 2 minutes.

TO ASSEMBLE THE CUPCAKES: Using a paring knife, cut a 1-inch divot from each cupcake and fill the whole with 1 tablespoon caramel. Replace the divot.

Fill the piping bag fitted with the open circle tip with the salted caramel buttercream. Pipe a large dollop of buttercream in the center of each cupcake and set aside.

Set up a decorating station for the witches' hats. Fill a medium bowl with the purple sanding sugar. Set a baking tray with parchment paper underneath the bowl, and a baking tray with parchment paper beside the bowl where you can set the witches' hats to dry.

Melt the candy melts along with the coconut oil according to package instructions and pour into a medium bowl.

Dip a separated chocolate sandwich cookie into the melted coating, shaking off any excess. Dip the cookie into the purple sanding sugar to coat. Set aside to dry completely.

Dip the mini ice cream sugar cones into the melted coating, shaking off any excess. Dip the sugar cones into the sanding sugar and roll around in the sanding sugar to adhere. Attach the mini cone to the cookie, pressing to stick. Cut slices of pink fondant for the witches' hat bands. Cut to size and wrap around the purple hats. Let hats harden enough to handle.

Place a purple witch's hat on top of each cupcake's buttercream dollop, pressing down to nestle into the buttercream and adhere.

— **Chapter 2** —

Perilous Pies
and
Sweet Scary
Bakes

Dr. Finkelstein Charlotte Royale Brain Cake

Who knew the brains behind Dr. Finkelstein's giant noggin could look this delicious? The Charlotte Royale cake is best served cold, like Dr. Finkelstein's ice cold heart! The brain-like design is created using a filled jelly cake roll, sliced and set around a creamy, delicious freeze-dried raspberry filling. Prepare this cake one day in advance to account for the various chilling times—the wait time will be worth it, as everyone will be clamoring for a slice of *this* brain!

Yield: About 14 servings | Skill Level: Moderate

FOR THE CAKE ROLL

1 cup cake flour
1 cup granulated sugar, divided
1 teaspoon baking powder
¾ teaspoon fine sea salt
½ cup vegetable oil
¼ cup whole milk
4 egg yolks, room temperature
1 tablespoon pure vanilla extract
6 egg whites, room temperature
¼ teaspoon cream of tartar
1½ cups raspberry jam

FOR THE FILLING

1 cup whole milk
1½ teaspoons vanilla bean paste
4 large egg yolks
⅔ cup granulated sugar
2 tablespoons gelatin powder
1½ cups heavy cream
⅛ teaspoon fine sea salt
1¼ cups freeze-dried raspberries

DECORATING INGREDIENTS AND TOOLS

One 8-by-2-inch round cake pan
One 12-by-18-inch rimmed Swiss roll baking sheet
Serrated knife
Offset spatula
One 3-quart round bowl
Plastic cling wrap
Cake platter

TO MAKE THE CAKE ROLL: Using nonstick cooking spray, grease and line an 8-by-2-inch round cake pan with parchment paper. Spritz the parchment paper again with more cooking spray. Spray your jelly roll (aka Swiss roll) rimmed baking sheet with nonstick cooking spray, line with parchment paper, spray the parchment paper, and dust lightly with flour.

Preheat the oven to 325°F.

In a large bowl, whisk together the cake flour, ¾ cup sugar, baking powder, and salt.

In a medium bowl, whisk together the vegetable oil, milk, egg yolks, and vanilla extract.

In the bowl of a stand mixer fitted with the whisk attachment or a large bowl with a handheld mixer, whip the egg whites on medium speed until frothy. Add the cream of tartar and continue whipping until soft peaks form. Continue whipping, adding the remaining sugar 1 teaspoon at a time. Beat on high speed until glossy and holding firm peaks.

Add the egg yolk mixture to the flour mixture, folding them together until smooth and incorporated, forming the beginning of the cake batter.

Carefully fold the egg white mixture into the cake batter in three gentle additions, being careful not to deflate the egg white mixture.

Divide the batter: Fill the 8-inch round cake pan with about 1½ cups cake batter. Pour the remaining batter onto the jelly roll pan, using an offset spatula to spread it evenly to the edges.

Bake the cakes for 13 to 16 minutes, until both cakes are lightly golden brown and spring back to the touch, keeping in mind that the jelly roll pan might be done sooner.

Remove cakes from the oven and let cool down to the touch.

Once the cakes are cooled, spread a thin layer of the raspberry jam on the entire surface of the jelly roll cake.

Working with the long edge of the cake, peel the parchment paper off as you roll the cake in a tight spiral. Once the cake is rolled, wrap it tightly in plastic cling wrap to hold its shape. Refrigerate for 1 hour to firm up for easier slicing!

CONTINUES ON PAGE 38

TO MAKE THE FILLING: In a medium saucepan over medium heat, simmer the milk and vanilla bean paste.

In a medium bowl, whisk the egg yolks and sugar to combine. Whisking constantly, slowly pour the hot milk mixture into the egg yolks, then return the milk and yolk mixture to the saucepan.

Cook over medium-high heat, stirring constantly with a wooden spoon, until the mixture thickens and coats the back of the spoon, about 4 minutes. Strain the custard into a bowl to smooth.

In a glass cup, stir and dissolve the gelatin with ⅓ cup cool water. Whisk the gelatin mixture into the still-hot custard. Cool the custard mixture so that it is cool to the touch but not firm.

In the bowl of a stand mixer fitted with the whisk attachment or a large bowl with a handheld mixer, whip the heavy cream to soft peaks. Using a whisk, carefully fold the whipped cream into the cooled custard mixture. Fold in the freeze-dried raspberries and ⅛ teaspoon of fine sea salt.

TO ASSEMBLE THE CHARLOTTE ROYALE: Line a rounded bowl with plastic cling wrap. Using a sharp or serrated knife, evenly slice the chilled raspberry cake roll into ½-inch-thick slices and line the entire bowl, nestling the jelly roll slices next to each other as tightly as possible without squishing their shape. Once the bowl is lined to the top, fill the center with the freeze-dried raspberry custard mixture. Nestle the 9-inch round cooled cake on top, trimming if needed. Cover completely with plastic cling wrap and refrigerate overnight to set.

To serve the brain cake, have a cake platter ready. Remove the cling wrap from the top of the bowl. Place the platter on top of the bowl and carefully but deftly flip the bowl and plate over, inverting the Charlotte Royale onto the plate. Carefully lift the bowl upward and carefully peel away the plastic cling wrap. Allow the oohing and aahing, then slice into wedges and serve!

Spiral Hill Poppy Seed Rolls

Inspired by the striking, curling pinnacle of Halloween Town's iconic Spiral Hill, these poppy seed rolls are soft, golden brown, and rolled with a sweet, nutty-crunch poppy seed paste filling. For an even more satisfying texture, sprinkle them with a touch of sanding sugar before putting them in the oven.

Yield: About 24 rolls | Skill Level: Easy

FOR THE DOUGH

1½ cups whole milk, lukewarm (98°F to 105°F)

1½ teaspoons active dry yeast

½ cup granulated sugar

2 tablespoons vegetable oil

3 tablespoons unsalted butter, melted

½ teaspoon fine sea salt

4½ cups all-purpose flour (plus more for dusting and rolling out rolls)

2 egg yolks, whisked, divided

1 cup sanding sugar (optional)

FOR THE POPPY SEED FILLING

1¾ cups poppy seeds, ground to make 1½ cups

1 cup honey

1 cup whole milk, room temperature

2 tablespoons fresh lemon juice

2 tablespoons granulated sugar

¾ teaspoon fine sea salt

1 teaspoon pure vanilla extract

DECORATING INGREDIENTS AND TOOLS

2 large baking pans

Offset spatula

TO MAKE THE DOUGH: In the bowl of a stand mixer fitted with the paddle attachment or a large bowl with a handheld mixer, combine the milk, yeast, and sugar, and allow to sit for 10 minutes. Add the vegetable oil, butter, and salt and mix to combine.

Swap out the paddle for the dough kneading hook. With the mixer on low speed, add the flour in ½-cup increments. Knead the dough on medium speed until elastic and non-sticky to the touch, 15 minutes. If dough seems too sticky, add ⅛ cup more flour.

TO MAKE THE POPPY SEED FILLING: In a medium saucepan over medium-high heat, combine the ground poppy seeds, honey, milk, lemon juice, sugar, and salt.

Bring to a low boil and allow to reduce, stirring often with a wooden spoon, until thickened and paste-like, 4 to 5 minutes. Stir in the vanilla extract and let cool completely.

TO ASSEMBLE THE ROLLS: Preheat the oven to 300°F. Line two large baking pans with parchment paper.

Dust your clean counter or workspace with flour. Using a rolling pin, roll out the dough to form a large rectangle, about 13 by 18 inches and ¼ inch thick.

Brush the dough surface with a thin layer of whisked egg yolk.

Use an offset spatula to spread an even layer of poppy seed filling on top of the dough, working from the middle outward toward the edges.

Roll the dough starting from the long edge working toward you, forming a thick, long roll.

Slice the dough into about 24 even pieces. Space the rolls evenly on the prepared baking pans, about 12 to a pan, allowing about 1 inch of space around each roll. Brush the top of each roll with egg yolk and sprinkle with sanding sugar, if desired.

Bake for 23 to 26 minutes, or until rolls are golden brown, puffed, and baked through.

Striped Skellington Suit Baked Coffee Donuts

Serve your friends in style with these scrumptious striped Jack Skellington coffee donuts! These donuts steal the show—they're dipped in dark chocolate ganache, piped with Jack's iconic pinstripes, and flaunt little fondant bow ties. Note: I use a piping bag to fill the donut baking pans for efficiency and even distribution, but it's optional! The ganache can be prepared even before the donuts, allowing it to thicken for a glaze while the donuts are baking.

Yield: 12 donuts | Skill Level: Easy

FOR THE DONUTS

¼ cup unsalted butter, room temperature, plus more for greasing donut pan

¼ cup vegetable oil

½ cup granulated sugar

⅔ cup golden brown sugar

2 large eggs

1½ teaspoons baking powder

¼ teaspoon baking soda

1 teaspoon ground nutmeg

¾ teaspoon fine sea salt

1 teaspoon coffee extract

1 teaspoon pure vanilla extract

2⅔ cups all-purpose flour

1 cup whole milk

FOR THE CHOCOLATE GANACHE

1 cup heavy cream

1 cup good-quality dark chocolate, chopped or in chips

FOR THE ROYAL ICING

2 cups icing sugar, sifted, plus more if needed

1½ tablespoons meringue powder

2½ tablespoons warm water

½ teaspoon pure vanilla extract

DECORATING INGREDIENTS AND TOOLS

2 donut baking pans

Large piping bag fitted with a large open circle tip (optional)

Black fondant

Large baking pan

Piping bag fitted with a small open circle tip

TO MAKE THE DONUTS: Preheat the oven to 400°F. Grease your donut baking pans.

In the bowl of a stand mixer fitted with the paddle attachment or a large bowl using a handheld mixer, beat together the butter, oil, granulated sugar, and brown sugar on high speed until smooth and creamy.

With the mixer on low speed, add the eggs one at a time, mixing to combine. Add the baking powder, baking soda, nutmeg, salt, coffee extract, and vanilla extract and mix to combine on low speed.

With the mixer still on low speed, alternate between adding the flour and adding the milk in three portions, beginning and ending with the flour, until just combined. Do not overmix.

Optional: Fill the piping bag fitted with the large open circle tip with donut batter. Pipe the batter into the donut pan cavities.

Bake the donuts for 8 to 10 minutes, until lightly browned and a toothpick inserted into the center of the donut comes out with only moist crumbs. Do not overbake!

Remove donut pans and allow to cool for a few minutes, then turn out donuts and let cool completely. Once cooled, work promptly to avoid exposing them to air for too long and drying out before they're dipped in ganache!

TO MAKE THE GANACHE: In a small saucepan over medium-high heat, bring the cream to a low boil. Remove the pan from the heat and add the chocolate, swirling the pan so the cream covers the chocolate entirely. Let sit for 10 minutes.

Slowly whisk the mixture together until smooth and glossy. Transfer to a bowl for dipping your donuts. Refrigerate to cool down and thicken mixture, about 10 minutes.

TO MAKE THE ROYAL ICING: In the bowl of a stand mixer fitted with the whisk attachment or a large bowl with a handheld mixer, beat the icing sugar, meringue powder, and water together at low speed to incorporate. Add the vanilla extract. Beat on high speed for about 10 minutes. If icing is too thin, add icing sugar 1 tablespoon at a time, until it is of thicker piping consistency that will hold the shape of Jack's suit stripes. Cover with a damp towel until ready to use.

TO ASSEMBLE THE DONUTS: Place a parchment paper–lined large baking pan under a wire rack for easy cleanup. Dip the cooled donut into the chocolate ganache, gently shaking off any excess, then place on the wire rack to dry. Continue with remaining donuts. Allow ganache to dry.

In the meantime, make 12 bow ties out of the black fondant. Shape the fondant into spider-like creature bow ties by creating 6 leg-shaped pieces. Top the leg pieces with a bat-shaped face in the center.

Fill the piping bag fitted with the small open circle tip with the royal icing.

Pipe white stripes on the dried chocolate ganache. Add a bow tie to each donut.

Man-Eating Wreath Giant Chocolate Chip Cookie

When Jack spreads his well-intentioned yet chaotic holiday cheer, Christmas Town wreaths come alive, scaring children all over town! But at least you can fight back against this particularly delicious Man-Eating Christmas Wreath by cutting it into pieces and eating it! Grease and flour the cake pan extremely well to ensure that your cookie pops out of its cake pan with ease!

Yield: 16 pieces | Skill Level: Easy

FOR THE GIANT CHOCOLATE CHIP COOKIE

3 cups all-purpose flour

1 teaspoon baking powder

½ teaspoon baking soda

1 teaspoon fine sea salt

1 cup unsalted butter, room temperature

¾ cup brown sugar

½ cup granulated sugar

¼ cup raw turbinado sugar

1 egg, room temperature

1 tablespoon pure vanilla extract

2 cups best-quality semisweet or dark chocolate callets or chips

FOR THE VANILLA BUTTERCREAM

2 cups unsalted butter, room temperature

4 cups icing sugar, sifted

2 teaspoons pure vanilla extract

Pinch of fine sea salt

Green gel food coloring

DECORATING INGREDIENTS AND TOOLS

One 12-inch round cake pan

Offset spatula

Cake platter or cake board

Piping bag fitted with an open star tip

Yellow candy melt disks or round yellow candy or yellow fondant

Two chocolate chips

White fondant or slivered almonds

Red fondant or red fruit leather

Red berry candies or red gumballs (optional)

TO MAKE THE COOKIE: Preheat the oven to 350°F. Grease and flour the entire 12-inch round cake pan's bottom and sides, line it with a piece of parchment paper cut to size, and spritz with nonstick cooking spray.

In a medium bowl, whisk to combine the flour, baking powder, baking soda, and salt and set aside.

In the bowl of a stand mixer fitted with the paddle attachment or a large bowl with a handheld mixer, beat the butter, brown sugar, granulated sugar, and turbinado sugar on high speed until doubled in volume and light and fluffy, about 2 minutes, scraping down the sides of the bowl as needed.

With the mixer on low speed, add the egg and the vanilla extract, mixing until combined.

With the mixer turned off, add the flour mixture to the bowl. Pulse to combine to avoid a dust storm; then mix on low speed until just incorporated, about 30 seconds.

Add the chocolate chips and pulse to combine until incorporated, about 10 seconds. Mix for another 15 to 20 seconds if needed to combine the cookie dough.

Turn the cookie dough out into the prepared cake pan. Using an offset spatula, spread the dough to the edges of the pan in an even layer.

Bake for 24 to 27 minutes, until the top and edges of the cookie are lightly browned. Let cool completely in the cake pan.

TO MAKE THE BUTTERCREAM: In the bowl of a stand mixer fitted with the paddle attachment or a large bowl with a handheld mixer, pulse the butter, icing sugar, vanilla, and salt to combine and mix on low speed to incorporate.

Increase to high speed and beat the buttercream until light and fluffy and doubled in volume, about 2 minutes. Add the green gel color and beat to incorporate.

CONTINUES ON PAGE 44

TO ASSEMBLE THE COOKIE: Prepare a cake platter or cake board by adding a dollop of buttercream to the center to help the cookie adhere. Turn the cookie out onto a large cutting board so that the flat side of the cookie is on top, then place the cake board, buttercream dollop side down, on top of the upside down cookie. Invert the cake board so the cookie is right side up.

Using an offset spatula, frost the cookie with a thin layer of green buttercream, leaving the center circle unfrosted. Fill the piping bag fitted with the open star piping tip with the remaining green buttercream. Pipe a wreath "leaf" border by piping green drop stars and rosettes nestled together on top of the cookie, again leaving the center empty (like a wreath hole!).

Use yellow candy melt disks or yellow fondant to make the evil eyes. Add two chocolate chips for irises, adhering with a dab of buttercream, or pipe in green irises with green buttercream.

Use white fondant cut into large teeth or use slivered almonds as teeth.

Create a red festive bow out of red fondant or red fruit leather. Dot the wreath with red berry candies or gumballs, if desired!

Christmas Town Cranberry Muffins

When the little children of Christmas Town wake up on Christmas morning to Halloween-festooned chaos, perhaps a warm-from-the-oven cranberry orange zest muffin might calm them down! Fragrant orange and tangy cranberries combine for a cozy holiday-friendly muffin. Serve warm with butter and jam!

Yield: 24 muffins | Skill Level: Easy

3 cups all-purpose flour

2 teaspoons baking powder

1 teaspoon baking soda

1 teaspoon fine sea salt

2 large oranges

2 cups granulated sugar

½ cup unsalted butter, melted

1 cup whole milk

2 large eggs

2 teaspoons pure vanilla extract

1½ cups fresh or thawed frozen cranberries

¾ cup dried cranberries

Preheat the oven to 400°F. Line two muffin tins with paper muffin liners.

In a large bowl, whisk to combine the flour, baking powder, baking soda, and salt.

In a separate large bowl, finely zest the oranges. Juice the oranges (about ½ cup orange juice) and add to the bowl. Add the sugar, butter, milk, eggs, and vanilla extract and whisk to combine.

Add the flour mixture to the orange mixture, folding together to combine. Add the fresh and dried cranberries, folding gently to combine.

Divide the batter evenly into the prepared muffin tins, filling ⅔ full. Bake 22 to 24 minutes, until golden brown and a toothpick inserted into the center comes out with only moist crumbs. Allow to cool slightly for 10 minutes, then serve warm!

Pumpkin King Pumpkin Pie

Behold the "master of fright and demon of light"—Jack Skellington, the Pumpkin King himself! This creamy, dreamy simple pumpkin pie works for Halloween, Christmas, *and* Thanksgiving, with a *Nightmare Before Christmas* twist! Note: This pie takes some time to set up in the refrigerator, so it's a perfect pie to make a day in advance, and finish with the face decor on the day of serving.

Yield: 12 slices | Skill Level: Easy

FOR THE GINGERSNAP CRUST

1¾ cups gingersnap crumbs
¼ cup packed brown sugar
1 tablespoon all-purpose flour
¾ teaspoon fine sea salt
¼ cup unsalted butter, melted

FOR THE PUMPKIN SUGAR FILLING

½ cup granulated sugar
½ cup all-purpose flour
½ cup packed brown sugar
1 cup whole milk
¾ cup heavy cream
2 teaspoons pure vanilla extract
¾ teaspoon fine sea salt
1 cup pumpkin puree
1 teaspoon ground cinnamon
1 teaspoon ground ginger
1 teaspoon ground nutmeg

FOR THE CHOCOLATE GANACHE

½ cup heavy cream
½ cup dark chocolate chips

FOR THE MAPLE WHIPPED CREAM

2 cups whipping cream
½ cup icing sugar, sifted
2 tablespoons pure maple syrup (or more, if desired)
Pinch of salt

DECORATING INGREDIENTS AND TOOLS

9-inch pie pan
Offset spatula
Piping bag fitted with a small open circle tip

TO MAKE THE CRUST: Preheat the oven to 350°F. Grease a 9-inch pie pan well with butter and dust with flour.

In a large bowl, whisk together the gingersnap crumbs, brown sugar, flour, and salt. Add the butter and mix to combine. Press the mixture evenly to the bottom and sides of the pie pan. Bake for 10 minutes to set; remove from the oven and let cool.

TO MAKE THE FILLING: In a medium bowl, whisk the granulated sugar and flour to combine. Add the brown sugar and mix to combine. Whisk in the milk, cream, vanilla extract, and salt and mix to combine. Carefully whisk in the pumpkin puree, cinnamon, ginger, and nutmeg.

TO ASSEMBLE THE PIE: Pour the pumpkin pie filling into the prepared gingersnap cookie crust. Bake for 30 to 32 minutes, until the filling is set yet still a touch jiggly. (Extra filling can be reserved for mini pies or baked in separate ramekins, and served with whipped cream.) Let cool, then refrigerate overnight to set.

TO MAKE THE GANACHE: In a small saucepan set on low heat, heat the cream to a low boil. Remove from heat and add the chocolate, swirling the pan to cover chocolate completely with the cream. Allow to sit for 10 minutes, then gently whisk to combine. Power-chill in the refrigerator or freezer for 30 to 60 minutes to thicken to a piping consistency.

CONTINUES ON PAGE 48

TO MAKE THE WHIPPED CREAM: In the bowl of a stand mixer fitted with the whisk attachment or a large bowl with a handheld mixer, whip the whipping cream on high speed until soft peaks form. Add the icing sugar, maple syrup to taste, and salt and whip further to thicken to stiff peaks.

Remove pie from fridge. Using a small offset spatula, dollop a generous amount of whipped cream onto the center of the pie. Using the offset spatula, spread the dollop into a large oval to resemble Jack Skellington's skull head. Smooth the whipped cream into an even layer. To assist with creating Jack's face, drag a toothpick through the whipped cream to draw the face on first, using this as a guide for piping the chocolate ganache.

Fill a piping bag with the thickened, cooled piping-consistency ganache. Pipe the outline for his large eyes, nostrils, and a smile. Add stitch lines to the smile. Fill in the eyes with the ganache and use an offset spatula to smooth to the edges of the eye outline.

Undersea Gal Fish-Scale Cheesecake Bars

Undersea Gal, one of Halloween Town's most unique residents, resembles some combination of a sea creature and a mermaid. Fully supportive of Jack's quest to celebrate Christmas, she dives headfirst into making his dream a reality. Inspired by her iconic green scales, these fish scale piped cheesecake bars are a perfect tribute to Undersea Gal! Note: You'll need to let these chill in the refrigerator, so make them one day ahead of serving.

Yield: 12 bars | Skill Level: Easy

FOR THE CHOCOLATE COOKIE CRUST
24 chocolate sandwich cookies
3 tablespoons unsalted butter, melted

FOR THE CHEESECAKE FILLING
2 cups (16 ounces) cream cheese, room temperature
1 cup granulated sugar
¼ cup heavy cream, room temperature
3 large eggs, room temperature
1 teaspoon pure vanilla extract
Green gel food coloring

FOR THE LEMON BUTTERCREAM
1½ cups unsalted butter, room temperature
3 cups icing sugar, sifted
1 tablespoon lemon juice
Pinch of salt
Gel food coloring in turquoise and green

DECORATING INGREDIENTS AND TOOLS
8-inch square baking pan
Plastic cling wrap
Small offset spatula
Piping bag fitted with a small open circle tip

TO MAKE THE CRUST: Preheat oven to 350°F. Grease and line an 8-inch square pan with a piece of parchment paper cut to overhang the pan (for easy removal of bars). Place the chocolate sandwich cookies in a resealable plastic bag and crush them using a rolling pin. In a small saucepan set over medium heat, melt the butter. In a small bowl, combine the crushed cookies and butter.

Press the mixture evenly into the bottom of the pan. Bake the crust for 10 minutes, then let cool completely on a wire rack. Leave the oven set to 350°F.

TO MAKE THE FILLING: In the bowl of a stand mixer fitted with the paddle attachment or a large bowl with a handheld mixer, beat the cream cheese and sugar on medium speed until combined, about 1 minute, scraping down the sides of the bowl as needed.

Add the heavy cream and beat on medium speed to combine. Turn the mixer to low speed, and add the eggs one at a time to incorporate. Add the vanilla extract and ¼ teaspoon of green food coloring and mix to combine. Pour the batter onto the cooled crust.

Bake until the center is no longer jiggly, and the edges are lightly golden brown, 35 to 40 minutes. Let it cool in the pan on a wire rack for about 30 minutes, then refrigerate overnight to completely chill and firm up.

TO MAKE THE BUTTERCREAM: In the bowl of a stand mixer fitted with the paddle attachment or a large bowl with a handheld mixer, beat the butter, icing sugar, lemon juice, and salt on low speed to incorporate. Increase to high speed and beat until doubled in volume and light and fluffy, about 2 minutes.

Divide the buttercream into two medium bowls. Using gel color, color one bowl with ¼ teaspoon of turquoise gel color, and the second bowl with ¼ teaspoon green gel color.

Place a piece of plastic cling wrap on the counter. Using a spatula, spread a thick log of turquoise buttercream in the center. Spread a thick log of green buttercream nestled right beside it. Roll up the plastic cling wrap into a larger log. Snip the end of the plastic cling wrap log and place cut side down into the piping bag fitted with the small open circle tip. Squeeze the piping bag; the two colors will combine as you pipe.

TO ASSEMBLE THE BARS: Carefully remove the cheesecake from the pan using the parchment paper overhang to assist, and place on a large cutting board. To get clean cheesecake bars, use a sharp knife that has been run under very hot water and wiped clean—wipe the knife clean after each cut to achieve clean cheesecake slices.

To pipe the buttercream scales, pipe a row of colored buttercream dollops on the back edge of the cheesecake bar, turning the piping bag slightly each time to vary the pattern of the colors being piped. Using an offset spatula, drag the spatula toward you, making a divot and "scale" shape in the buttercream. Pipe the next row of dollops overlapping the last row of piped and shaped divots, continuing until you reach the end of the cheesecake bar, making your cheesecake bar "scaly"! Repeat the process for each cheesecake bar. Store in the refrigerator in an airtight container until serving.

Lock, Shock, and Barrel Mini Cake Trio

Lock, Shock, and Barrel, the sneaky, cunning little trio you hate to love, come to life in these delicious mini cakes. These three trick-or-treating, mischievous rascals wreak havoc when they kidnap Sandy Claws and drop him into Oogie Boogie's lair! Lock's little red devil cake, Shock's green-faced witch cake, and Barrel's skeleton mask cake make a terrifically tantalizing trio! Dive into this project with two other friends, and you can each take on making "three of a kind, birds of a feather—now and forever!"

Yield: 3 mini cakes | Skill Level: Moderate

FOR THE LEMON-LIME CAKES

1½ cups whole milk

2 teaspoons lemon juice

3 cups cake flour

1 tablespoon baking powder

1 teaspoon baking soda

1 teaspoon fine sea salt

1 cup unsalted butter, room temperature

2 cups granulated sugar

4 large eggs, room temperature

1 teaspoon pure lemon extract

Zest of one lemon

Zest of one lime

FOR THE VANILLA BUTTERCREAM

2 cups unsalted butter, room temperature

4 cups icing sugar, sifted

1 tablespoon pure vanilla extract

Pinch of salt

DECORATING INGREDIENTS AND TOOLS

Three 6-by-2-inch round cake pans

Three 7-inch round cake boards or cake plates

Red, mint green, dark gray, and bright green gel food coloring

Cake scraper

White fondant

Red fondant

Wooden skewers cut to size

Black fondant

Paring knife

Purple fondant

Circular bottom edge of a small piping tip

Small round cookie cutter or circular bottom edge of a large piping tip

2 piping bags, each fitted with a multi-opening tip

TO MAKE THE CAKES: In a liquid measuring cup, add the milk and lemon juice and whisk to combine to create a buttermilk. Set aside for 10 minutes to thicken.

In a large bowl, whisk together the cake flour, baking powder, baking soda, and salt.

Preheat the oven to 350°F. Grease and line the cake pans with parchment paper cut to size.

In the bowl of a stand mixer fitted with the paddle attachment or a large bowl with a handheld mixer, beat the butter and sugar on high speed until light and fluffy and doubled in volume, about 2 minutes, scraping down the sides of the bowl as needed.

Add the eggs one at a time, mixing on low speed to incorporate after each addition.

Add the lemon extract, lemon zest, and lime zest, mixing on low speed to combine.

Add the flour mixture in three additions, alternating with the lemon milk mixture, beginning and ending with the flour mixture. Mix on low speed to combine to form a smooth batter, 30 to 60 seconds total.

Divide the batter evenly among the three cake pans. Bake for 20 to 22 minutes, until lightly golden and a toothpick inserted in the center comes out with only moist crumbs. Let cool completely on wire racks before using.

TO MAKE THE BUTTERCREAM: In the bowl of a stand mixer fitted with the paddle attachment, beat the butter, icing sugar, vanilla extract, and salt on low speed to incorporate. Increase to high speed and beat until light and fluffy and doubled in volume, about 2 minutes.

TO ASSEMBLE THE CAKES: Prepare all the individual components for each mini cake. Lay out cake boards or cake plates for building the cakes. Divide the buttercream: a bowl with 1¼ cups of buttercream for Lock's red gel coloring, a bowl with 1¼ cups of buttercream for Shock's mint green gel coloring, and a bowl with 1¼ cups of uncolored buttercream for Barrel's face. Place remaining buttercream in two smaller bowls; tint one dark gray-black for Shock's hair, and one bright green for Barrel's hair.

CONTINUES ON PAGE 54

Place the Lock cake on one of the cake boards. Crumb-coat frost the Lock cake with red buttercream. Place the Shock cake on a second cake board. Crumb-coat frost the Shock cake with mint green buttercream. Place the Barrel cake on the third cake board. Crumb-coat frost the Barrel cake with the uncolored buttercream. Chill in the fridge or freezer for 15 minutes to firm up the buttercream. Remove from the fridge and apply a second coat of red buttercream to the Lock cake, a second coat of mint green buttercream to the Shock cake, and a second coat of uncolored buttercream to the Barrel cake, using a cake scraper for each cake to create a smooth finish.

TO MAKE LOCK'S FEATURES: Using the white fondant, mold sharp little white teeth. Mold two thick devil's ears out of red fondant. Insert a trimmed wooden skewer into each ear to anchor into the cake. Mold a devil's nose for Lock. Using the black fondant, shape two black eyes in an almond shape for Lock. Roll out the black fondant to ¼ inch thick and, using a paring knife, cut out an open-mouthed smile shape.

TO MAKE SHOCK'S FEATURES: Mold a purple witch's hat using the purple fondant. Insert a wooden skewer to anchor the hat onto the cake. Add a tiny amount of mint green gel food coloring to a piece of white fondant, kneading it to incorporate the color and using cornstarch to keep it dry as necessary. Mold a long triangle shape for Shock's witch nose. Using the white fondant, shape two almond shapes for Shock's witch eyes. Using the bottom edge of a small piping tip, punch out small black fondant circle irises for Shock's eyes. Assemble the whites of the eyes with the black irises. Using the piping bag fitted with the green buttercream, pipe strands of buttercream for Shock's short haircut, overlaying as needed.

TO MAKE BARREL'S FEATURES: Roll out the white fondant and cut out an oval shape about 5 inches in diameter for Barrel's mask. Using a 1- to 2-inch circle-shape cookie cutter or a large piping tip bottom edge, punch out two eye holes. Using a paring knife, cut out two skull-like nostrils and cut out a sinister smile. Mold little white rectangles for Barrel's teeth. Using a small piping tip bottom edge, cut white fondant for the whites of Barrel's eyes. Roll a thick ball of white fondant about 2 inches wide. Cut in half; insert trimmed wooden skewer into each piece for Barrel's ears to anchor the ears into the cake. Roll out the black fondant to ¼ inch thick and, using a 1- to 2-inch circle-shape cookie cutter or a large piping tip bottom edge, punch out two circles for Barrel's skull holes. Cut out a black mouth shape for Barrel's skull mouth. Punch out small black fondant circle irises for Barrel's eyes. Assemble the whites of the eyes with the black irises. Using the piping bag fitted with the black buttercream, pipe long overlaying squiggles of buttercream to create Barrel's hair.

Face of Evil Lemon Meringue Pie

This pie is an Oogie Boogie–inspired lemon meringue delight, piled high "to the brim with fright!" Dig into this cool lemon pie, topped with green-tinted billowy Swiss meringue and popping with Oogie Boogie's mischievous face! Tangy lemon filling and a marshmallow cloud of meringue make this a pie perhaps Oogie Boogie himself would love!

Yield: One 9-inch pie | Skill Level: Moderate

FOR THE PIE CRUST

1¼ cups all-purpose flour
½ teaspoon fine sea salt
½ cup unsalted butter, cold and cut into small pieces
⅛ cup ice water
1 egg, whisked, for egg wash

FOR THE LEMON PIE FILLING

5 large egg yolks
¼ cup cornstarch
1¼ cups granulated sugar
¼ teaspoon fine sea salt
1¼ cups water
¾ cup fresh lemon juice
3 tablespoons lemon zest
4 tablespoons butter, unsalted

FOR THE SWISS MERINGUE

7 large egg whites
¾ cup granulated sugar
¼ teaspoon cream of tartar
¼ teaspoon fine sea salt
Green gel food coloring

DECORATING INGREDIENTS AND TOOLS

9-inch pie pan
Pie baking weights or dried beans
Plastic cling wrap
Round chocolate callets or chocolate disks
Thin chocolate biscuit sticks (such as Pocky chocolate sticks), the cookie parts cut off and the chocolate parts cut into even-size pieces
Candy thermometer

TO MAKE THE PIE CRUST: In the bowl of a food processor, pulse to combine the flour and salt. Add the cold butter and pulse to combine, until mixture resembles coarse crumbs with some larger pieces of butter remaining, about 10 seconds. With the food processor running, slowly drizzle the ice water in, about 1 tablespoon at a time, noting that you may not need the entire ⅛ cup—until dough combines and holds together but is not wet and sticky.

Prepare a large section of plastic cling wrap. Plop the pie dough onto the cling wrap and close the cling wrap up into a round disk shape, gently shaping the dough into place, wrapping the dough completely and creating a flattened disk. Refrigerate for 2 hours to firm up, or overnight.

After the dough has chilled, bring the disk out and place on a clean work surface dusted lightly with flour. Roll out the pie dough to about ¼ inch thick, and place into the pie pan, pressing in evenly. Crimp the edges. Chill in freezer for 15 minutes, until firm, while you preheat the oven to 425°F.

To blind-bake the crust, place parchment paper onto your chilled pie dough and fill the pan with pie baking weights or dried beans. Bake for 20 minutes. Remove the pie crust from the oven, and remove the parchment paper and baking weights. Brush the pie with egg wash and place back into the oven to bake for another 10 minutes. Reduce the oven temperature to 375°F and bake until golden brown, 15 to 20 minutes more. Remove from the oven and cool pie crust on a wire rack.

CONTINUES ON PAGE 56

TO MAKE THE FILLING: In a medium bowl, whisk the egg yolks and set aside.

In a medium saucepan over medium-high heat, whisk to combine the cornstarch, sugar, salt, and water. Bring to a low boil, whisking constantly, until the mixture thickens slightly. Remove from heat.

Temper the egg yolks—this means adding the hot cornstarch mixture a little at a time to the yolks, to avoid cooking the yolks. Whisk in half of the cornstarch mixture to the egg yolks, one spoonful at a time.

Return the egg yolk/cornstarch mixture to the medium saucepan and whisk to combine, stirring constantly over medium-high heat, cooking for 3 to 4 minutes.

Remove from heat and stir in the lemon juice, lemon zest, and butter, whisking to combine to a smooth filling. Return the saucepan to the stove to heat up again once the meringue is almost ready.

TO MAKE THE MERINGUE: In the metal bowl from a stand mixer or a large metal bowl, whisk to combine the egg whites, sugar, cream of tartar, and salt. Set the bowl over a small saucepan filled ¼ full with low-boiling water. Heat the mixture until the sugar is dissolved, stirring and scraping down the sides of the bowl as needed with a heatproof spatula, until a digital thermometer registers 160°F, to pasteurize the mixture.

Return the metal bowl to the stand mixer, fitted with the whisk attachment, or use a handheld mixer. Whip the mixture on high speed until the meringue begins to form soft peaks. Add a tiny amount of green gel coloring at this point. Continue whipping on high speed until the meringue is billowy and glossy, 5 to 8 minutes.

TO ASSEMBLE THE PIE: Add the hot lemon filling to the baked and cooled pie crust. Add the meringue onto the top of the pie, with the intention of creating a raised, tall peak in the center to resemble Oogie Boogie. You can use a kitchen blowtorch to toast the meringue, or leave as is to keep the green color more intact!

Insert two chocolate disks into the meringue for Oogie's eyes. Carefully press in the chocolate biscuit sticks in a zigzag pattern to form his mouth. Serve immediately.

Zero the Dog Gingerbread Doghouse

Jack's best friend, Zero, is arguably the cutest resident of Halloween Town! And it just so happens to be Zero's glowing nose that leads the way through a foggy night so Jack may deliver his well-intentioned ghoulish gifts on Christmas! When he's not saving the day (or night), Zero's got his own cool home: a doghouse sitting in Halloween Town's cemetery. This gingerbread doghouse is decorated in haute Halloween style, perfect for Zero.

Yield: 1 gingerbread house | Skill Level: Advanced

FOR THE GINGERBREAD

1 cup unsalted butter, room temperature

1 cup granulated sugar

1 cup molasses

1 teaspoon fine sea salt

½ teaspoon baking soda

1 teaspoon ground cinnamon

1 teaspoon ground ginger

5 cups all-purpose flour

FOR THE ROYAL ICING

7 cups (1 kilogram bag) icing sugar

¾ cup merlngue powder

Pinch of salt

¾ cup water

1 teaspoon pure vanilla extract

DECORATING INGREDIENTS AND TOOLS

2 to 6 large baking sheets

Plastic cling wrap

Bone-shaped cookie cutter

Coffin cookie cutter

Dachshund cookie cutter (or free-form cookie)

Orange and black gel food coloring

3 piping bags, each fitted with a small open circle tip

Piping bag fitted with a medium open circle tip

Sharp paring knife, for cutting shapes, if needed

Orange round hard candies for windows and Zero's nose (optional)

TO MAKE THE GINGERBREAD: In the bowl of a stand mixer fitted with the paddle attachment or a large bowl with a handheld mixer, beat the butter, sugar, molasses, salt, baking soda, cinnamon, and ginger on medium-high speed, scraping down the sides of the bowl as needed. Beat until lightened in color, fluffy, and doubled in volume, about 2 minutes.

Add the flour 1 cup at a time, pulsing to combine, scraping down the sides of the bowl as needed. Mix on low speed for a few seconds to incorporate the dough, adding 1 tablespoon of water as needed if too crumbly.

Divide the dough into four sections, turning the sections out onto individual pieces of plastic cling wrap. Flatten and shape the dough into disks and wrap tightly with cling wrap. Refrigerate for 1 hour, or overnight. (Chilling the dough helps it keep its shape when baking.)

Remove the dough from the refrigerator after chilling. Prepare 2 large baking sheets with parchment paper or silicone baking mats.

Cut out 2 pieces for the front and back; each piece should be 5 inches wide, 5 inches tall, and the roof part 4 inches tall. Cut out two 5½-inch square roof pieces. Cut out two 5-inch square side pieces.

Using the sharp knife, cut out a cross for Zero's doghouse topper. Using cookie cutters, cut out bone cookie shapes, a coffin, and a dachshund. Using your fingers, add more pieces to the dog's nose and ears to elongate them to look like Zero.

Preheat the oven to 350°F and prepare 2 to 6 large baking sheets with parchment paper. Place the cut-out pieces on the baking sheets. If you have room in your freezer, you can freeze the pieces again for 15 minutes to help maintain their shape before baking. Remove from freezer.

Bake cookies for 10 to 15 minutes depending on the shapes you're using—keep an eye on the gingerbread and bake until lightly browned. Allow cookie pieces to cool completely before assembling your house.

CONTINUES ON PAGE 58

TO MAKE THE ICING: In the bowl of a stand mixer fitted with the paddle attachment or a large bowl with a handheld mixer, mix the icing sugar, meringue powder, and salt on low speed until combined. Add the water and vanilla extract, mixing on medium-high speed until thickened, glossy, and bright white.

Divide the royal icing into three portions. Tint 1 cup of royal icing orange using 1 teaspoon of orange gel food coloring for Halloween-y doghouse flair, tint 1 cup of royal icing black using 2 teaspoons black gel food coloring, and keep the remaining icing white.

Use immediately or cover them with a damp towel to prevent them from drying out.

Have fun decorating Zero's doghouse to your cold heart's content!

Decorate the house pieces while still flat. Once everything is completely dry, assemble the pieces. Use a piping bag fitted with a small open circle tip and filled with white royal icing to line the peak of the roof, the sides of the roof, and the sides of the front and back of Zero's house.

Using a piping bag fitted with a small open circle tip and filled with white royal icing, pipe the outline for the Zero the dog cookie. Pipe some royal icing into a small bowl and add a dribble of water to loosen it; use a spoon to spoon it onto the Zero cookie to "fill" the cookie outline. Let dry completely. Do the same process with any bone cookies. Fill a piping bag fitted with a small open circle tip with black royal icing and pipe "zero" on the front of the doghouse above where the door will go. Pipe the outline of the cross cookie, and pipe the outline for the coffin door, and fill it with the black icing as you did above. Let coffin door dry completely. Using the white royal icing, pipe Zero's skull and crossbones on top. Pipe two black eyes onto Zero's skull. Let dry completely. Pipe Zero's eyes, mouth, and details onto the white cookie. Add the orange candy nose using a dot of royal icing to adhere. Let dry completely.

Fill a piping bag fitted with a small open circle tip with orange royal icing, and pipe shingles on the roof pieces. Let dry completely. Optional: Alternate with orange, black, and white icing on the roof shingles.

Assemble the doghouse using a piping bag fitted with a medium open circle tip filled with the white royal icing. Pipe lines of royal icing on your cake board where your house pieces will sit. Place the front house piece into the royal icing. Pipe a line of royal icing to the inside edges of the front house piece and attach the side pieces. Hold in place until dried and secure, shimmying it into place if needed and using more royal icing to glue as needed. Attach the back of the dog house in the same fashion. Let dry completely and firmly, about 20 minutes. Pipe the edges of the front of the house, sides of the house, and back of the house. Carefully add the first roof side and hold until dried and secure, about 10 minutes. Add the second roof side, using more royal icing to glue and secure as needed. Gently move the second roof piece to evenly match the first roof piece, if needed. Hold in place until dried and secure, about 10 minutes. Don't worry if the royal icing gushes out the sides, you can add piped royal icing dots along the seams of the house, if needed.

Adhere the black doghouse door with royal icing. Hold it in place for 1 minute to dry a bit and stick. Use royal icing to attach the cross, and to create any further details. Lean the Zero dog cookie up against the doghouse.

— **Chapter 3** —

Frightful CooKies

Cockroach Citrus Madeleines

These creepy-crawly cookies, inspired by the hair-raising cockroaches of Halloween Town, make delightfully ghoulish treats! The real trick here is that they taste delicious, despite their icky appearance. You can use any color candy melts, but rust red will give the madeleines a more realistic cockroach appearance. Get ready for an infestation on your dessert table! Note: You can prepare the candy melts and decorating ingredients while the madeleines cool on wire racks, then assemble the treats once the madeleines are cooled.

Yield: 24 cookies | Skill Level: Easy

FOR THE MADELEINES
½ cup unsalted butter
¾ cup all-purpose flour
½ cup finely ground almond flour
½ cup plus 2 tablespoons granulated sugar
2 tablespoons lemon zest
½ teaspoon pure lemon extract
3 large eggs
¾ teaspoon fine sea salt

DECORATING INGREDIENTS AND TOOLS
Plastic cling wrap
Two 12-mold madeleine pans
Piping bag fitted with a large open circle tip
Two 12-ounce bags candy melts, one in burgundy or brown (or color of your choice) and one in black
2 teaspoons coconut oil, divided
Soft caramels or licorice

TO MAKE THE MADELEINES: In a small saucepan over low heat, melt the butter. Set aside to cool.

In a large bowl, whisk together the all-purpose flour, almond flour, and sugar.

Add the lemon zest and lemon extract to the cooled butter, mixing to combine. In a separate large bowl, combine the eggs with the salt, whisking until frothy. Carefully whisk in the flour mixture to combine, then fold in the butter mixture to combine. Cover the bowl with plastic cling wrap and refrigerate until chilled, or overnight.

Preheat the oven to 350°F. Grease the madeleine pans with butter, then dust with flour to prevent sticking. Fill a piping bag fitted with a large open circle tip with the batter. Pipe the batter into each mold, filling each cavity half full. Bake until the edges of the madeleines are lightly golden brown, 12 to 14 minutes. Turn out onto wire racks while they cool.

TO ASSEMBLE THE COCKROACHES: Prepare each of the candy melts and 1 teaspoon coconut oil according to the package instructions. Place the burgundy candy melts in a small bowl. Set a wire rack atop a baking sheet lined with parchment paper, to catch any drips for easy cleanup.

Dip ⅔ of one end of a madeleine into the burgundy candy melts for the cockroach's body, and place on wire rack. Add cut-up caramel or licorice legs to the body, sticking them to the candy melts.

Using a piping bag fitted with a small open circle tip, add the black candy melts to the piping bag. Pipe an outline of the cockroach head onto the bare madeleine, then pipe to fill. Add caramel antennae; use a toothpick to dot two burgundy eyes on top of the black.

Let dry completely before serving!

Sally Patchwork Cookie Hearts

Lovestruck Sally is made from patched-up parts stitched together and stuffed with dead leaves, a creation in response to Dr. Finkelstein's yearning for companionship. Using a fun patchwork method of combining colors of cookie dough, these cotton candy–flavored cookies may very well end up being the heart of your sweets table! If you can't find cotton candy extract, you can use pure almond extract instead.

Yield: 18 to 24 cookies | Skill Level: Easy

FOR THE COTTON CANDY COOKIES

3 cups all-purpose flour

2 teaspoons baking powder

¾ teaspoon fine sea salt

1 cup unsalted butter, room temperature

1¼ cups granulated sugar

2 large eggs, room temperature

1 teaspoon cotton candy extract

1 teaspoon pure vanilla extract

DECORATING INGREDIENTS AND TOOLS

Turquoise, fuchsia, and yellow gel food coloring

Plastic cling wrap

2 large baking sheets

Heart-shaped cookie cutter

TO MAKE THE COOKIES: In a large bowl, whisk together the flour, baking powder, and salt to combine.

In the bowl of a stand mixer fitted with the paddle attachment or a large bowl with a handheld mixer, beat the butter and sugar on high speed until light and fluffy and doubled in volume, about 2 minutes. Scrape down the sides of the bowl as needed.

Add the eggs, cotton candy extract, and vanilla extract, beating on low speed to combine.

With the mixer turned off, add the flour mixture to the butter mixture. Pulse to combine, then beat on low speed to incorporate and form a cookie dough.

Divide the dough into three equal portions.

Wearing food-safe gloves and using parchment paper to protect your countertop from staining, color each portion with a different color, using ½ teaspoon each of turquoise, fuchsia, and yellow gel. Wrap each piece in plastic cling wrap and chill for 30 minutes in the refrigerator.

Preheat the oven to 350°F. Line two large baking sheets with parchment paper. Prepare a lightly floured work surface for creating the cut-out patchwork hearts.

Remove the colored doughs from the refrigerator and roll them out to equal sizes of ¼-inch thickness, about 10 inches round. Pull apart into small pieces of varying sizes to create a marbled patchwork look.

TO MAKE THE PATCHWORK DOUGH: On the prepared work surface, place the dough pieces so that they overlap slightly, essentially making a large rectangular sheet of overlapping cookie dough patchwork squares. Lightly flour your rolling pin and run it gently on top of all the pieces to make one connected sheet of multicolored dough. Using the heart cookie cutter, cut out heart cookie shapes as close together as possible to maximize the rolled-out dough, and place on prepared baking sheets. Chill for 15 minutes in the freezer, if desired, to help the cookies hold their shape.

Bake cookies for 8 to 10 minutes, or until lightly browned on edges and set. Let cookies cool completely on their baking sheets.

Worm's Wort and Frog's Breath Soup Bowl Cookies

Nothing is more suspicious than Frog's Breath! When Sally makes soup for Dr. Finkelstein, she pulls a fast one on him: By adding deadly nightshade, she makes Dr. Finkelstein fall fast asleep, allowing Sally to escape her tower. This special Worm's Wort and Frog's Breath Soup in cookie form won't put *you* to sleep, but it will keep your guests begging for more as they bite into these herbaceous rosemary-tinged lemon cookies.

Yield: 18 to 24 cookies | Skill Level: Easy

FOR THE ROSEMARY LEMON COOKIES

3 cups all-purpose flour

1 teaspoon baking powder

1 teaspoon fine sea salt

1 cup granulated sugar

1 tablespoon lemon zest

2 tablespoons finely minced fresh rosemary, plus more for decorating (optional)

1 cup unsalted butter, room temperature

1 large egg, room temperature

1 teaspoon pure lemon extract

FOR THE LEMON ROYAL ICING

7 cups icing sugar, sifted, plus more if needed

5 tablespoons meringue powder

1 teaspoon pure lemon extract

¼ to ½ cup water

DECORATING INGREDIENTS AND TOOLS

Plastic cling wrap

2 large baking sheets

Large circle-shaped cookie cutter

Sharp paring knife

Lime green and black gel food coloring

3 piping bags fitted with small open circle tips

White circle sprinkles (optional)

TO MAKE THE COOKIES: In a medium bowl, whisk to combine the flour, baking powder, and salt. Set aside.

In a small bowl use clean hands to massage the sugar, lemon zest, and rosemary together, releasing the lemon oils and imparting flavor to the sugar, until the sugar appears light yellow in color and the three ingredients have been thoroughly incorporated.

In the bowl of a stand mixer fitted with the paddle attachment or a large bowl with a handheld mixer, beat the butter and lemon-herb sugar on high speed until light and fluffy and doubled in volume, about 2 minutes. Scrape down the sides of the bowl as needed.

With the mixer on low speed, add the egg and lemon extract, mixing to combine.

With the mixer turned off, add the flour mixture to the butter mixture. Pulse to combine, then mix on low speed until incorporated and a dough forms, about 30 seconds.

Divide the dough into two disks. Wrap with plastic cling wrap and refrigerate for 2 hours, or overnight.

Preheat oven to 350°F. Line two large baking sheets with parchment paper. Lightly flour a work surface.

Roll out the cookie dough evenly to about ¼ inch thick. Using the large circle cookie cutter, cut out 9 to 12 circles. Using a sharp paring knife, cut the cookies in half to form half-circles to resemble soup bowls. Place the cookie on the prepared baking sheets. Freeze the baking sheets with the unbaked cookies for 15 minutes to firm up before baking, if desired.

Bake for 8 to 10 minutes, until lightly golden brown and edges are set. Let cool completely on wire racks before frosting.

TO MAKE THE ROYAL ICING: In the bowl of a stand mixer fitted with the paddle attachment or a large bowl with a handheld mixer, beat the icing sugar, meringue powder, lemon extract, and ¼ cup water on low speed to combine. Increase the speed to medium-high and whip until fluffy and dense, 5 to 7 minutes. Add a small dribble of water at a time, if too thick; if too thin, add icing sugar 1 tablespoon at a time to thicken. Use immediately, or cover with a damp towel to prevent drying out.

Reserve a small amount of white royal icing for the soup "highlight," and divide the rest into two medium bowls and one small bowl. Place one cup of royal icing in the first bowl and tint with ½ teaspoon lime green gel coloring. Place one cup of royal icing in the second bowl and tint it with ¼ teaspoon black gel color to make a gray color for creating the look of the soup bowl. In the small bowl, fill with ½ cup royal icing and add two teaspoons or more of black gel color for creating the outlines of the cookie.

Fill a piping bag fitted with a small open circle tip with green icing. Pipe the outline for the soup, an almond-like oval shape. Repeat for all the cookies. Pipe out the remaining royal icing into a bowl and add a tiny dribble of water to loosen it (if you loosen it too much, add icing sugar to thicken). Spoon the royal icing into the soup outline, spreading to the edges, for all the cookies.

Fill another piping bag fitted with a small open circle tip with gray icing. Pipe the outline for the soup bowl, a boat-like shape underneath the green soup. Repeat for all the cookies. Do the same method for filling the gray bowl as above.

Before the green soup dries completely, add white circle sprinkles as soup "highlight."

Let cookies dry completely.

Fill the third piping bag with the black royal icing and pipe an outline around the soup bowl and the soup itself, adding a few tiny dots onto the soup for pepper, if desired.

Sally Blue Helping Hands Cookies

Sally is made of many different patchwork pieces, which comes in handy when problems arise and help is needed! Her leg kicks out to distract Oogie Boogie from his dreadful taunting of Sandy Claws, and Sally's helping hands attempt to come to Sandy Claws's rescue—so don't be surprised to see these cookies spider-skitter off their plate!

Yield: 18 to 24 cookies | Skill Level: Easy

FOR THE LEMON ZEST HAND COOKIES

3 cups all-purpose flour

2 teaspoons baking powder

¾ teaspoon fine sea salt

1 cup unsalted butter, room temperature

1½ cups granulated sugar

1 egg, room temperature

1 tablespoon lemon zest

1 teaspoon pure lemon extract

FOR THE LEMON ROYAL ICING

7 cups icing sugar, sifted, plus more if needed

5 tablespoons meringue powder

1 teaspoon pure lemon extract

¼ to ½ cup water

DECORATING INGREDIENTS AND TOOLS

Plastic cling wrap

2 large baking sheets

Hand-shaped cookie cutter

Sky blue and fuchsia gel food coloring

2 piping bags fitted with small open circle tips

TO MAKE THE COOKIES: In a medium bowl, whisk to combine the flour, baking powder, and salt. Set aside.

In the bowl of a stand mixer fitted with the paddle attachment or a large bowl with a handheld mixer, beat the butter and sugar on high speed until light and fluffy and doubled in volume, about 2 minutes. Scrape down the sides of the bowl as needed.

With the mixer on low speed, add the egg, lemon zest, and lemon extract, mixing to combine.

With the mixer turned off, add the flour mixture to the butter mixture. Pulse to combine, then mix on low speed until incorporated and a dough forms, about 30 seconds.

Divide the dough into two disks. Wrap with plastic cling wrap and refrigerate for 2 hours, or overnight.

Preheat oven to 350°F. Line two large baking sheets with parchment paper. Lightly flour a work surface.

Roll out the cookie dough evenly to about ¼ inch thick. Using the hand-shape cookie cutter, cut out cookie hands, evenly arranging on the prepared baking pans, 12 per pan. Freeze for 15 minutes to firm up the dough to help hold the cookies' shape, if desired.

Bake for 8 to 10 minutes, until cookies are lightly golden brown, fragrant, and set. Cool completely on wire racks.

TO MAKE THE ICING: In the bowl of a stand mixer fitted with the paddle attachment or a large bowl with a handheld mixer, beat the icing sugar, meringue powder, lemon extract, and ¼ cup of water on low speed to combine. Increase the speed to medium-high and whip until fluffy and dense, 5 to 7 minutes. Add a small dribble of water at a time, if too thick; if too thin, add icing sugar 1 tablespoon at a time to thicken. Use immediately, or cover with a damp towel to prevent drying out.

TO ASSEMBLE THE COOKIES: Divide the royal icing into a medium bowl and a small ¼-cup bowl. Add 1½ cups to the first bowl and tint with 1 teaspoon of the sky blue gel coloring. Add ½ teaspoon of fuchsia gel coloring to a small ¼-cup bowl of royal icing for Sally's fingernails.

Fill a piping bag fitted with a small open circle tip with the blue icing. Pipe a thin outline all the way around the hand. Repeat for all the cookies. Pipe out the remaining blue royal icing into a bowl and add a tiny dribble of water to loosen it (if you loosen it too much, add icing sugar to thicken). Spoon the royal icing into the hand outline, spreading to the edges. Let dry completely.

Fill the second piping bag fitted with a small open circle tip with fuchsia icing. Add little dots of fingernail polish to each hand. Repeat for all the cookies.

Lavender Earl Grey Butterfly Cookies

In an attempt to help, Sally sends up a bottled gift to Jack, and when he opens it, to his delight, a lovely mist billows out and blossoms into a ghostly butterfly before his eyes! Inspired by that moment, these Lavender Earl Grey Butterfly Cookies will enchant you with their herbal, tea-essence flavor, perfect when dipped into a cup of fragrant milky tea.

Yield: 18 to 24 cookies | Skill Level: Easy

FOR THE LAVENDER EARL GREY COOKIES
1 cup unsalted butter

Loose tea from 4 Earl Grey tea bags (or ¼ cup loose-leaf Earl Grey tea)

1½ cups granulated sugar

¼ teaspoon finely ground food-grade lavender

2½ cups all-purpose flour

1 teaspoon fine sea salt

1 large egg, room temperature

1 teaspoon pure vanilla extract

DECORATING INGREDIENTS AND TOOLS
Plastic cling wrap

2 large baking sheets

Butterfly-shaped cookie cutter

TO MAKE THE COOKIES: In a small saucepan over medium heat, melt the butter. Add the loose Earl Grey tea leaves, remove from the heat, and let the flavor infuse the butter for 10 minutes. Strain the butter into a small bowl using a fine mesh strainer and discard the tea leaves. Little bits of tea will be in the butter, which is totally fine. Refrigerate to solidify to room temperature, about 20 minutes.

In a small bowl, using your fingers, rub together the sugar and food-grade lavender, releasing the oils and flavor from the lavender.

In a medium bowl, whisk the flour and salt to combine and set aside.

In the bowl of a stand mixer fitted with the paddle attachment or a large bowl with a handheld mixer, beat the tea butter and lavender sugar on high speed until light, fluffy, and doubled in volume, about 2 minutes. Scrape down the sides of the bowl as needed. With the mixer on low speed, add the egg and vanilla extract and mix to combine.

With the mixer turned off, add the flour mixture to the butter mixture. Pulse to combine, then mix to incorporate until a dough forms, about 30 seconds.

Divide the cookie dough into two flat disks. Wrap in plastic cling wrap and refrigerate for 2 hours, or overnight.

Preheat oven to 350°F. Line two large baking sheets with parchment paper. Lightly flour a work surface.

Roll out the cookie dough to about ¼-inch thickness. Cut out butterfly cookies and place evenly on prepared baking sheets. Freeze for 15 minutes, if desired, to firm up the dough to help hold the cookies' shape.

Bake for 8 to 10 minutes, until cookies are lightly golden brown, fragrant, and set. Cool completely on wire racks.

Spiral Hill Moon Cookies

At the top of the graveyard in Halloween Town, Spiral Hill is the pinnacle of the cemetery, where the yellow moon shines brightly on Jack Skellington's bone-white skull. These cookies, inspired by Spiral Hill and swirled with black sesame tahini, are the perfect picnic food for a clear, crisp night at the local burial grounds!

Yield: About 36 cookies | Skill Level: Easy

FOR THE BLACK SESAME TAHINI

½ cup toasted black sesame seeds

Pinch of fine sea salt

1 tablespoon vegetable oil

1 tablespoon honey

FOR THE BLACK SESAME SWIRL COOKIES

2 cups all-purpose flour

½ teaspoon baking powder

¾ teaspoon fine sea salt

1 cup unsalted butter, room temperature

¾ cup icing sugar

2 teaspoons whole milk

1 large egg

1 teaspoon pure orange extract

¼ cup toasted black sesame tahini

¼ cup toasted black sesame seeds

¼ cup turbinado sugar

1 egg, lightly beaten

TO MAKE THE TAHINI: In a food processor, blend the black sesame seeds, salt, vegetable oil, and honey until a paste forms, about 1 minute.

TO MAKE THE COOKIES: In a medium bowl, whisk to combine the flour, baking powder, and salt. Set aside.

In the bowl of a stand mixer fitted with the paddle attachment or a large bowl with a handheld mixer, beat the butter and sugar on high speed until light and fluffy, scraping down the sides of the bowl as needed.

Add the milk, egg, and orange extract, mixing on low speed to combine.

With the mixer turned off, add the flour mixture, pulsing to combine. Increase to low speed and mix until incorporated, about 30 seconds. Turn the mixer off and remove half the dough from the mixer.

To the remaining half in the mixer, add the ¼ cup of black sesame tahini and mix until incorporated and the mixture's color deepens, 15 seconds.

Lightly flour a sheet of parchment paper at your workspace. Place the uncolored piece of dough on top, then top with another piece of parchment paper to prevent the sticking of dough as you roll it out. Roll on top of the parchment paper, rolling out the dough to a rectangle shape with about ⅛-inch thickness.

Repeat with the black sesame dough.

Place each flattened, parchment paper–covered piece on a baking sheet in the fridge or freezer and refrigerate until firm, about 20 minutes.

Lightly flour a work surface. Line two large baking sheets with parchment paper. Prepare a smaller baking sheet with parchment paper. In a small bowl, mix together the additional black sesame seeds and turbinado sugar and pour onto the center of the smaller baking sheet.

Remove the two flattened doughs from the fridge. Remove the parchment paper. Place the plain dough onto the floured work surface and place the black sesame dough directly on top, trimming away any extra dough to make them even. Starting from the long side, tightly roll the two doughs together to form a log. Trim any excess dough at the ends and cut the dough log in half. Wrap each log in plastic wrap, then refrigerate both logs in the fridge until firm, 20 to 30 minutes.

Remove the cookie dough logs from the fridge. Preheat oven to 350°F.

Brush each log half with the beaten egg, and roll each log carefully in the black sesame/turbinado sugar mixture on the smaller baking sheet. Slice the log into evenly sized cookies, about ¼-inch thick circles, and evenly distribute them on the prepared baking sheets.

Bake cookies for 12 to 14 minutes, until lightly golden and set. Remove from oven and let cool completely on wire racks.

Toffee Espresso Coffin Cookies

While vampires are known for sleeping during the daytime, these coffee-infused toffee espresso cookies might just jolt them out of their coffins, and just in time for the Mayor of Halloween Town's annual celebration speech! The coffin cookie is also a nod to Jack's unique choice of transportation—a coffin sled to help deliver his macabre gifts!

Yield: 18 to 24 cookies | Skill Level: Easy

FOR THE TOFFEE ESPRESSO COOKIES

1½ tablespoons instant espresso powder

3 tablespoons boiling water

3 cups all-purpose flour

2 teaspoons baking powder

1 teaspoon fine sea salt

1 cup unsalted butter, room temperature

1 cup granulated sugar

1 large egg, room temperature

2 teaspoons pure vanilla extract

½ cup toffee bits, chopped finely

FOR THE COFFEE BUTTERCREAM

1½ cups unsalted butter, room temperature

3 cups icing sugar, sifted

1 teaspoon pure coffee extract

Pinch of salt

DECORATING INGREDIENTS AND TOOLS

Plastic cling wrap

2 large baking sheets

Coffin-shaped cookie cutter

Fuchsia and black gel food coloring

2 piping bags fitted with small open circle tips

Offset spatula

Piping bag fitted with a small open star tip

Pearl or other little round candies (optional)

TO MAKE THE COOKIES: In a glass, mix together the espresso powder and boiling water to dissolve.

In a medium bowl, whisk to combine the flour, baking powder, and salt. Set aside.

In the bowl of a stand mixer fitted with the paddle attachment or a large bowl with a handheld mixer, beat the butter and sugar on high speed until light, fluffy, and doubled in volume, about 2 minutes. Scrape down the sides of the bowl as needed.

With the mixer on low speed, add the egg, prepared espresso, and vanilla extract, mixing to combine.

With the mixer turned off, add the flour mixture to the butter mixture. Pulse to combine, then mix on low speed until incorporated and a dough forms, about 30 seconds.

Divide the dough into two disks. Wrap with plastic cling wrap and refrigerate for 2 hours, or overnight.

Preheat oven to 350°F. Line two large baking sheets with parchment paper. Lightly flour a work surface.

Roll out the cookie dough evenly to about ¼ inch thick. Using the coffin cookie cutter, cut out coffin cookies, evenly arranging on the prepared baking pans, 12 per pan. Freeze for 15 minutes, if desired, to firm up the dough to help hold the cookies' shape.

Bake for 8 to 10 minutes, until cookies are lightly golden brown, fragrant, and set. Cool completely on wire racks.

TO MAKE THE BUTTERCREAM: In the bowl of a stand mixer fitted with the paddle attachment or a large bowl with a handheld mixer, beat the butter, icing sugar, coffee extract, and salt on low speed to incorporate. Increase to high speed and beat until light, fluffy, and doubled in volume, about 2 minutes.

CONTINUES ON PAGE 74

TO ASSEMBLE THE COOKIES: Reserved 2 cups of the buttercream for piping the coffin, and divide the rest into two small bowls. Add 1 cup of buttercream to one bowl and add ¼ teaspoon fuchsia gel color. Add 1 cup of buttercream to the other bowl and add 1 teaspoon black gel color.

Place some of the uncolored coffee buttercream into a piping bag fitted with a small open circle tip. Pipe an outline of the coffin. Fill the inside with buttercream. Using an offset spatula, smooth the buttercream, being careful not to mess up the defining outline. Repeat on all the cookies. Chill the cookies for 15 minutes to set the buttercream. Add the black-tinted buttercream to the second piping bag fitted with an open circle tip. Pipe a coffin outline, nails, and "RIP" on the coffin box, if desired. Fill the piping bag fitted with the open star tip with the fuchsia buttercream. Pipe flowers around the coffin. Finish the flowers with little pearl candies, if desired.

RIP Gravestone Chocolate Sugar Cookies

Rest in pieces—chocolate sugar cookie pieces, that is! The Halloween Town graveyard is overflowing with homes for ghostly residents, including Jack's best friend, Zero. Customize these gravestone cookies, inspired by those tombstones seen in the film, with silly or creepy names piped on with black edible marker or black royal icing.

Yield: 18 to 24 cookies | Skill Level: Easy

FOR THE CHOCOLATE COOKIES

1½ cups all-purpose flour
¾ cup Dutch-process cocoa powder
1 teaspoon baking powder
¾ teaspoon fine sea salt
¾ cup unsalted butter, room temperature
1 cup granulated sugar
1 large egg, room temperature
1 teaspoon pure vanilla extract

FOR THE ROYAL ICING

7 cups icing sugar, sifted, plus more if needed
5 tablespoons meringue powder
1 teaspoon pure vanilla extract
¼ to ½ cup water

DECORATING INGREDIENTS AND TOOLS

Plastic cling wrap
2 large baking sheets
Gravestone cookie cutter
Black gel food coloring
2 piping bags fitted with small open circle tips

TO MAKE THE COOKIES: In a medium bowl, whisk together the flour, cocoa powder, baking powder, and salt to combine.

In the bowl of a stand mixer fitted with the paddle attachment or a large bowl with a handheld mixer, beat the butter and sugar on high speed until light and fluffy and doubled in volume, about 2 minutes, scraping down the sides of the bowl as needed.

Add the egg and vanilla extract and mix on low speed to combine.

With the mixer turned off, add the flour mixture to the wet ingredients. Pulse to combine, then mix on low speed to incorporate until a cookie dough forms, about 30 seconds.

Divide the dough into two disks and wrap in plastic cling wrap. Refrigerate for 2 hours, or overnight.

Preheat the oven to 350°F. Line two large baking sheets with parchment paper. Prepare a lightly floured work surface.

Remove the dough from the refrigerator and roll it out to about ¼-inch thickness on the prepared work surface. Using the cookie cutter, cut out gravestones and place 9 to 12 on each of the prepared baking sheets. Freeze for 15 minutes if desired, to help keep the shape.

Bake for 8 to 10 minutes, until lightly brown and set. Let cool on wire racks.

TO MAKE THE ROYAL ICING: In the bowl of a stand mixer fitted with the paddle attachment or a large bowl with a handheld mixer, beat the icing sugar, meringue powder, vanilla extract, and ¼ cup water on low speed to combine. Increase the speed to medium-high and whip until fluffy and dense, 5 to 7 minutes. Add a small dribble of water at a time, if too thick; if too thin, add icing sugar 1 tablespoon at a time to thicken. Use immediately, or cover with a damp towel to prevent drying out.

TO ASSEMBLE THE COOKIES: Divide the royal icing. In one bowl, tint the royal icing gray by using a toothpick's tip of black gel coloring. If piping black royal icing for lettering, in another bowl, tint a small amount of icing black.

Fill a piping bag fitted with a small open circle tip with the gray royal icing. Pipe an outline around the gravestone. Repeat for each cookie. Pipe some royal icing into a small bowl and add a dribble of water to loosen it. Use a spoon to spoon it onto the gravestone to "fill" the cookie outline. Repeat for each cookie. Let dry completely.

Once dry, add the black "RIP" lettering, or use black edible marker to write out a name or message!

Chocolate Almond Eyeball Cookies

Leering eyeballs are popping around every corner in Halloween Town. Whether it's Dr. Finkelstein's watchful eye trailing Sally's every move, or the Cyclops's eye popping out of its socket, there's an eye for everyone! And even Halloween Town surely has ghoulishly foul residents with dietary restrictions—these gluten-free chocolate almond sugar cookies might just do the trick!

Yield: 18 to 24 cookies | Skill Level: Easy

FOR THE CHOCOLATE ALMOND COOKIES
2 cups finely ground almond flour
½ cup coconut flour
½ cup Dutch-process cocoa powder
1 teaspoon baking powder
1 teaspoon fine sea salt
½ cup unsalted butter, room temperature
1 cup granulated sugar
2 large eggs
2 teaspoons pure vanilla extract

FOR THE VANILLA CREAM CHEESE FROSTING
½ cup cream cheese, room temperature
1 cup unsalted butter, room temperature
3 cups icing sugar, sifted
1 teaspoon pure vanilla extract
Pinch of salt

DECORATING INGREDIENTS AND TOOLS
Plastic cling wrap
2 large baking sheets
Circle-shaped cookie cutter
Red gel food coloring
Piping bag fitted with a small open circle tip
Piping bag fitted with a large open circle tip
Small offset spatula
Chocolate disks

TO MAKE THE COOKIES: In a medium bowl, whisk to combine the almond flour, coconut flour, cocoa powder, baking powder, and salt. Set aside.

In the bowl of a stand mixer fitted with the paddle attachment or a large bowl with a handheld mixer, beat the butter and sugar on high speed until light and fluffy and doubled in volume, about 2 minutes. Scrape down the sides of the bowl as needed.

With the mixer on low speed, add the eggs and vanilla extract, mixing to combine.

With the mixer turned off, add the flour mixture to the butter mixture. Pulse to combine, then mix on low speed until incorporated and a dough forms, about 30 seconds.

Divide the dough into two disks. Wrap with plastic cling wrap and refrigerate for 2 hours, or overnight.

Preheat oven to 350°F. Line two large baking sheets with parchment paper. Lightly flour a work surface.

Roll out the cookie dough evenly to about ¼ inch thick. Using the circle cookie cutter, cut out eyeball cookies, arranging them evenly on the prepared baking pans, 12 per pan. Freeze for 15 minutes, if desired, to firm up the dough to help hold the cookies' shape.

Bake for 8 to 10 minutes, until cookies are lightly golden brown, fragrant, and set. Cool completely on wire racks before frosting.

TO MAKE THE FROSTING: In the bowl of a stand mixer fitted with the paddle attachment or a large bowl with a handheld mixer, beat the cream cheese, butter, icing sugar, vanilla extract, and salt on low speed to combine. Increase to medium speed and beat until thick and creamy.

TO ASSEMBLE THE COOKIES: Place a small amount of the frosting into a small bowl and color it with red gel food coloring. Fill the piping bag fitted with the small open circle tip with the red frosting.

Fill the piping bag fitted with the large open circle tip with the uncolored frosting and pipe a large dollop of cream cheese frosting in the center of each cookie. Using a small offset spatula, squash down the blob to create an eyeball shape.

Using the red frosting, start in the center and pipe squiggly lines for bloodshot eyes, working your way outward.

Place a chocolate disk at the center of the red bloodshot eye lines.

Toasted Hazelnut Bat Cookies

Bats are everywhere in Halloween Town—as common as a city crow—their bat wings spread wide as they glide past the bright yellow moon. Your guests might very well go batty for these scrumptious dark chocolate frosting-piped toasted hazelnut cookies! Note: Make your own toasted hazelnut flour by purchasing skinned, roasted hazelnuts. Grind to a fine meal (but not so much that it becomes a paste).

Yield: 18 to 24 cookies | Skill Level: Easy

FOR THE HAZELNUT COOKIES

1 cup toasted hazelnut flour made from
2 cups roasted, skinned hazelnuts
2½ cups all-purpose flour
1 teaspoon fine sea salt
1 cup unsalted butter, room temperature
1 cup granulated sugar
2 large eggs, room temperature
1 teaspoon pure vanilla extract
1 tablespoon hazelnut extract

FOR THE DARK CHOCOLATE FROSTING

¼ cup Dutch-process cocoa powder
¼ cup boiling water
1½ cups unsalted butter, room temperature
½ cup icing sugar, sifted, plus more if needed
½ teaspoon fine sea salt
2 cups dark chocolate, melted and cooled completely

DECORATING INGREDIENTS AND TOOLS

Plastic cling wrap
2 large baking sheets
Bat-shaped cookie cutter
Piping bag fitted with a very small open star tip
Red candies

TO MAKE THE COOKIES: In a medium bowl, whisk together the hazelnut flour, all-purpose flour, and salt.

In the bowl of a stand mixer fitted with the paddle attachment or a large bowl with a handheld mixer, beat the butter and sugar on high speed until light, fluffy, and doubled in volume, about 2 minutes. Scrape down the bowl as needed.

With the mixer on low speed, add the eggs, the vanilla extract, and the hazelnut extract.

Turn off the mixer. Add the flour mixture to the butter mixture and pulse to combine. Increase to low speed and mix until incorporated and a dough forms, about 30 seconds.

Divide the dough into two disks. Wrap with plastic cling wrap and refrigerate for 2 hours, or overnight.

Preheat oven to 350°F. Line two large baking sheets with parchment paper. Lightly flour a work surface.

Roll out the cookie dough evenly to about ¼ inch thick. Using the bat cookie cutter, cut out bat cookies, arranging evenly on the prepared baking pans, 12 per pan. Freeze for 15 minutes, if desired, to firm up the dough to help hold the cookies' shape.

Bake for 8 to 10 minutes, until cookies are lightly golden brown, fragrant, and set. Cool completely on wire racks before frosting.

TO MAKE THE FROSTING: In a small bowl, combine the cocoa powder and boiling water, stirring to dissolve.

In the bowl of a stand mixer fitted with the paddle attachment or a large bowl with a handheld mixer, beat the butter, icing sugar, and salt on low speed to combine. Increase speed to medium-high speed and beat until light and fluffy.

Reduce speed to low, adding the melted and cooled chocolate. Beat until combined, scraping down the sides of the bowl as needed. Add the cocoa powder mixture and beat until incorporated. Beat for 1 minute more to aerate. If the frosting is too loose to pipe, add more icing sugar, 1 tablespoon at a time, until slightly thicker, being careful not to oversweeten.

TO ASSEMBLE THE COOKIES: Add the chocolate frosting to the piping bag fitted with the small open star tip. Pipe the entire bat with little drop stars, nestling the stars close together. Adorn with two red candy eyes. Repeat with remaining cookies!

Halloween Town Christmas Tree Cookies

In Christmas Town, Jack discovers the strangeness of this brand-new-to-him holiday—not only the sounds of holiday joy and cheer, but decorations like he's never seen, including lush Christmas trees decorated with all the colorful holiday trimmings! These buttercream-piped Christmas tree cookies are decorated with a mixture of bones and baubles, bats and berries to make the ultimate Halloween Town/Christmas Town cookie!

Yield: 18 to 24 cookies | Skill Level: Easy

FOR THE VANILLA BEAN COOKIES

3 cups all-purpose flour

2 teaspoons baking powder

¾ teaspoon fine sea salt

1 cup unsalted butter, room temperature

1½ cups granulated sugar

1 egg, room temperature

1 tablespoon vanilla bean paste or seeds from 1 vanilla bean pod

1 teaspoon pure vanilla extract

FOR THE VANILLA BEAN BUTTERCREAM

2 cups unsalted butter, room temperature

4 cups icing sugar, sifted

1 tablespoon vanilla bean paste or seeds from 1 vanilla bean pod

Pinch of salt

DECORATING INGREDIENTS AND TOOLS

Plastic cling wrap

2 large baking sheets

Christmas tree–shaped cookie cutter

3 piping bags, each fitted with a small open star tip

Green and orange gel food coloring

Bone and skull sprinkles/candies

Mini chocolate-coated candies

Bat sprinkles

TO MAKE THE COOKIES: In a medium bowl, whisk to combine the flour, baking powder, and salt. Set aside.

In the bowl of a stand mixer fitted with the paddle attachment or a large bowl with a handheld mixer, beat the butter and sugar on high speed until light, fluffy, and doubled in volume, about 2 minutes. Scrape down the sides of the bowl as needed.

With the mixer on low speed, add the egg, vanilla bean paste, and vanilla extract, mixing to combine.

With the mixer turned off, add the flour mixture to the butter mixture. Pulse to combine, then mix on low speed until incorporated and a dough forms, about 30 seconds.

Divide the dough into two disks. Wrap with plastic cling wrap and refrigerate for 2 hours, or overnight.

Preheat the oven to 350°F. Line two large baking sheets with parchment paper. Lightly flour a work surface.

Roll out the cookie dough evenly to about ¼ inch thick. Using the Christmas tree cookie cutter, cut out cookie trees, arranging evenly on the prepared baking pans, 12 per pan. Freeze for 15 minutes to help hold the cookies' shape, if desired.

Bake for 8 to 10 minutes, until cookies are lightly golden brown, fragrant, and set. Cool completely on wire racks.

TO MAKE THE BUTTERCREAM: In the bowl of a stand mixer fitted with the paddle attachment or a large bowl with a handheld mixer, beat the butter, icing sugar, vanilla bean paste, and salt on low speed to incorporate. Increase to high speed and beat until light, fluffy, and doubled in volume, about 2 minutes.

TO ASSEMBLE THE COOKIES: Add ½ cup plain white buttercream to a piping bag fitted with an open star tip. In a small bowl, tint ½ cup buttercream orange. Add the orange buttercream to another piping bag fitted with an open star tip. Tint the rest of the buttercream with the green gel coloring and put it in the third piping bag.

Pipe the entire cookie with green buttercream drop stars, following the lines of the tree boughs. Add long swags of orange and white buttercream, then decorate with skull, bones, baubles (coated chocolate candies), and bats. Repeat with all the cookies.

— Chapter 4 —

Shuddersome Sheet Cakes

Chocolate Peppermint Ghost Sheet Cake

Throughout Halloween Town, many ghosts and ghouls float around the town square going about their daily business! This escapee from Halloween Town's cemetery may seem scary but is actually a simple chocolate peppermint sheet cake! The friendly specter cake will have your fellow ghouls and guests gasping with gustatory glee!

Yield: 1 cake, 15 to 20 servings | Skill Level: Easy

FOR THE CHOCOLATE PEPPERMINT SHEET CAKE

2 cups cake flour

2 cups granulated sugar

¾ cup Dutch-process cocoa powder

2 teaspoons baking soda

1 teaspoon baking powder

1 teaspoon fine sea salt

1 cup buttermilk

½ cup vegetable oil

2 large eggs

2 teaspoons pure vanilla extract

1 cup strong hot coffee

FOR THE CHOCOLATE BUTTERCREAM

1 cup unsalted butter, room temperature

1¾ cups icing sugar, sifted, plus more if needed

¼ cup Dutch-process cocoa powder

1 teaspoon pure vanilla extract

Pinch of salt

FOR THE PEPPERMINT BUTTERCREAM

1 cup unsalted butter, room temperature

2 cups icing sugar, sifted

1 teaspoon pure peppermint extract

Pinch of salt

DECORATING INGREDIENTS AND TOOLS

9-by-13-inch cake pan

Piping bag fitted with a large open circle tip

Small offset spatula

Piping bag fitted with a small open circle tip

TO MAKE THE CAKE: Preheat the oven to 350°F. Generously spray the entire cake pan with cooking spray or vegetable oil, then line the bottom with parchment paper cut to size. Spritz the parchment paper.

In a medium bowl, whisk together the flour, sugar, cocoa powder, baking soda, baking powder, and salt.

In the bowl of a stand mixer fitted with the paddle attachment or a large bowl with a handheld mixer, mix together on low speed the buttermilk, vegetable oil, eggs, and vanilla until combined.

With the mixer turned off, add the flour mixture to the buttermilk mixture, pulsing to combine, then mix on low speed until just combined, adding the hot coffee in a slow stream. Mix on low speed to combine, about 1 minute, scraping down the sides of the bowl as needed.

Pour the batter into the prepared cake pan and bake for 35 to 40 minutes, until the cake is springy to the touch and a toothpick inserted into the center of the cake comes back with only moist crumbs. While the cake is still warm, gently press down onto it using a sheet of parchment paper to level the cake's top surface, if desired.

Cool completely in the pan on a wire rack before frosting.

TO MAKE THE CHOCOLATE BUTTERCREAM: In the bowl of a stand mixer fitted with the paddle attachment or a large bowl with a handheld mixer, beat the butter, icing sugar, cocoa powder, vanilla, and salt on low speed to combine. Increase to high speed and beat until light, fluffy, and doubled in volume, about 2 minutes. Reserve ¼ cup of chocolate buttercream for piping details.

TO MAKE THE PEPPERMINT BUTTERCREAM: In the bowl of a stand mixer fitted with the paddle attachment or a large bowl with a handheld mixer, beat the butter, icing sugar, peppermint extract, and salt on low speed to combine. Increase to high speed and beat until light, fluffy, and doubled in volume, about 2 minutes.

TO ASSEMBLE THE CAKE: Turn the chocolate sheet cake out onto a cake board, or frost in the cake pan, if desired. Using the chocolate buttercream, frost a thick, even layer over the entire cake. Refrigerate until firm, about 20 minutes.

Fill the piping bag with the large open circle tip with the peppermint buttercream. Pipe the outline of a classic ghost onto the top of the cake. Pipe the rest of the peppermint buttercream to fill the center. Use the offset spatula to smooth the piping entirely. Fill the piping bag with the small open circle tip with the reserved ¼ cup of chocolate buttercream. Pipe two dollops for eyes, using a clean offset spatula to press down to flatten. Pipe a ghostly grimacing mouth.

Sally Buttercream Roses Sheet Cake

Sally loves flowers, especially when plucking petals for a game of He Loves Me, He Loves Me Not. This buttercream rosette piped cake in dark, beautiful colors would surely make Sally swoon—no potions required! Frost a thin layer of strawberry jam underneath the buttercream for a jammy surprise and extra strawberry flavor. Note: To achieve deep, dark yet bright colors, use a larger-than-usual amount of gel food coloring.

Yield: 1 cake, 15 to 20 servings | Skill Level: Moderate

FOR THE STRAWBERRY SHEET CAKE

¼ cup freeze-dried strawberries

2¾ cups cake flour

2 teaspoons baking powder

½ teaspoon baking soda

1 teaspoon fine sea salt

¾ cup vegetable oil

1¾ cups granulated sugar

4 large eggs

1½ cups pureed strawberries

1 teaspoon pure vanilla extract

FOR THE VANILLA BUTTERCREAM

2 cups unsalted butter, room temperature

4 cups icing sugar, sifted

2 teaspoons pure strawberry extract, or pure vanilla extract

Pinch of salt

DECORATING INGREDIENTS AND TOOLS

9-by-13-inch cake pan

Serrated knife

Strawberry jam (optional)

Dark green, fuchsia, violet, royal blue, and black gel food coloring

Piping bag fitted with a small leaf tip

3 piping bags fitted with medium open star tips

TO MAKE THE CAKE: Preheat the oven to 350°F. Generously spray the entire cake pan with cooking spray or vegetable oil, then line the bottom with parchment paper cut to size. Spritz the parchment paper and set aside.

In the bowl of a food processor, process the freeze-dried strawberries into a powder. In a large bowl, whisk together the cake flour, strawberry powder, baking powder, baking soda, and salt.

In the bowl of a stand mixer fitted with the paddle attachment or a large bowl with a handheld mixer, mix together on low speed the vegetable oil, sugar, eggs, strawberry puree, and vanilla extract.

With the mixer turned off, add the flour mixture to the oil mixture. Mix on low speed to combine until the batter just comes together, about 30 seconds, scraping down the sides of the bowl as needed.

Pour the batter into the prepared cake pan. Bake for 35 to 40 minutes, until lightly golden and a toothpick inserted into the center of the cake comes out with only moist crumbs.

Let cool completely before frosting.

TO MAKE THE BUTTERCREAM: In the bowl of a stand mixer fitted with the paddle attachment or a large bowl with a handheld mixer, beat the butter, icing sugar, strawberry extract, and salt on low speed to combine. Increase to high speed and beat until light, fluffy, and doubled in volume, about 2 minutes.

TO ASSEMBLE THE CAKE: Carefully turn the sheet cake out onto a cake board or cake platter. Trim and level the cake with a serrated knife to achieve an even top layer, if desired. Frost the cake with a thin layer of strawberry jam, if using.

Frost the entire cake with a very thin layer of vanilla buttercream. Retain ¼ cup of buttercream in a small bowl and add about ½ teaspoon gel food coloring to tint it dark green. Fill the piping bag fitted with the leaf tip with the green buttercream. Divide the rest of the buttercream in three—color one bowl with 1 teaspoon of fuchsia gel color, the second bowl with 1 teaspoon of violet gel color, and the third bowl with ¾ teaspoon of royal blue and ¼ teaspoon of black gel color. Mix each bowl to achieve desired color. Fill each piping bag fitted with the open star tip with one color.

Pipe rosettes all along the top of the cake. Holding the piping bag at a 90 degree angle, start in the center of your rosette, and pipe a counterclockwise swirl in two rotations, pulling up to finish. Repeat all over the cake. Fill any spaces or gaps with green piped leaves, and drop stars in various colors

Evil Lair Neon Tie-Dye Sheet Cake

Things get a little hairy down in Oogie Boogie's underground lair when Sandy Claws becomes his prisoner. Sandy is used to calming Christmas decor and cheer, but here he is met with fluorescent flashes of wild patterns and colors to blind him into fright, much to Oogie Boogie's delight! This neon-colored tie-dye cake decorated with zigzags and swirls in garishly ghoulish colors would fit right into the Oogie Boogie chaos!

Yield: 1 cake, 15 to 20 servings | Skill Level: Easy

FOR THE LEMON COCONUT SHEET CAKE

3 cups all-purpose flour

2 teaspoons baking powder

½ teaspoon baking soda

1 teaspoon fine sea salt

1 cup melted coconut oil

½ cup full-fat sour cream

3 large eggs

1½ cups granulated sugar

1 tablespoon lemon zest

½ cup lemon juice

1 tablespoon pure vanilla extract

⅔ cup full-fat coconut milk

FOR THE VANILLA BUTTERCREAM

2 cups unsalted butter, room temperature

4 cups icing sugar, sifted

2 teaspoons pure vanilla extract

Pinch of salt

DECORATING INGREDIENTS AND TOOLS

9-by-13-inch cake pan

Electric pink, neon green, electric purple, and yellow gel food coloring

2 piping bags fitted with open star tips

Cake board or cake platter

Chopstick

Serrated knife (optional)

Offset spatula

Candy skulls (optional)

Candy bugs (optional)

Gummy worms (optional)

TO MAKE THE LEMON COCONUT CAKE: Preheat the oven to 350°F. Generously spray the entire cake pan with cooking spray or vegetable oil, then line the bottom with parchment paper cut to size. Spritz the parchment paper and set aside. Prepare three medium bowls to divide the batter for coloring.

In a large bowl, whisk to combine the flour, baking powder, baking soda, and salt.

In the bowl of a stand mixer fitted with the paddle attachment or a large bowl with a handheld mixer, beat together on medium speed the coconut oil, sour cream, eggs, sugar, lemon zest, lemon juice, and vanilla.

With the mixer on low speed, add the flour mixture in three additions, alternating with the coconut milk, beginning and ending with the flour mixture, until a smooth batter forms, about 1 minute. Scrape down the sides of the bowl as needed.

Divide the batter into three bowls and tint each bowl with a different color— electric pink, neon green, and electric purple.

Pour blobs of the different colored batters into the pan to cover and fill the entire pan, with some colors overlapping others. To create the swirl tie-dye pattern, run a chopstick in a figure-eight motion through the batters, but do it only two to three times to retain the individual colors and the tie-dye effect. Tap the cake pan on the counter to level the batter and bake for 30 to 35 minutes, until the cake is lightly browned and a toothpick inserted into the center comes out with only moist crumbs.

CONTINUES ON PAGE 88

TO MAKE THE BUTTERCREAM: In the bowl of a stand mixer fitted with the paddle attachment or a large bowl with a handheld mixer, beat the butter, icing sugar, vanilla extract, and salt on low speed to combine. Increase to high speed and beat until light, fluffy, and doubled in volume, about 2 minutes.

TO ASSEMBLE THE CAKE: Place ½ cup of buttercream into each of 2 bowls. Tint one bowl electric pink and one bowl bright yellow. Fill the piping bags fitted with the open star tips, each with one color.

Tint the remaining buttercream bright neon green.

Turn the cake out onto a cake board or cake platter. Trim and level the cake using a serrated knife, if desired. Using an offset spatula, frost the entire top of the cake with a thick layer of neon green buttercream, smoothing to flatten. Refrigerate for 20 minutes to set.

Using the piping bags fitted with the open star tips, alternate piping yellow psychedelic swirls with electric pink zigzags all across the cake, to represent the chaos and color of Oogie Boogie's lair. Add little skull candies, bug candies, and gummy worms, if desired.

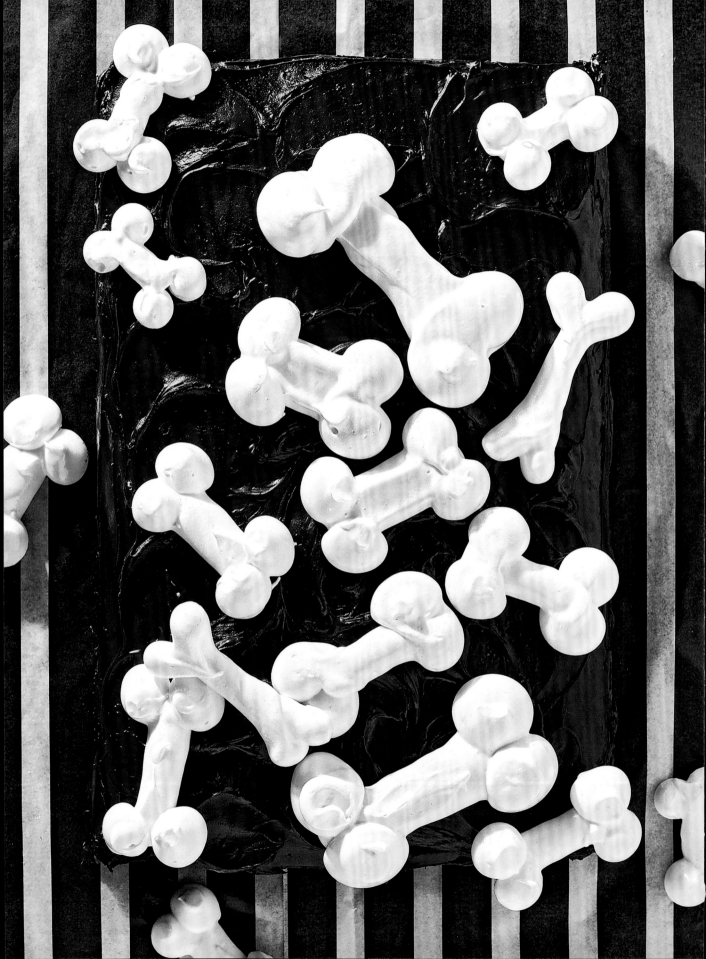

Marshmallow Meringue Skeleton Bones Sheet Cake

Jack will do anything for his best friend, Zero—including removing his own rib bone for a friendly game of catch! Make your own bones to throw onto a delicious dark chocolate, ganache-frosted sheet cake—light, airy, crisp meringue skeleton bones, of course! *Bone* appétit! Note: Make the bones the evening before so they can dry completely overnight.

Yield: 1 cake, 15 to 20 servings | Skill Level: Moderate

FOR THE MERINGUE BONES

½ lemon
½ cup egg whites (about 4 large egg whites)
1 cup granulated sugar
1 teaspoon pure vanilla extract

FOR THE CHOCOLATE CAKE

2½ cups all-purpose flour
1¼ cups Dutch-process cocoa powder
2 cups granulated sugar
2 teaspoons baking soda
1 teaspoon baking powder
1 teaspoon fine sea salt
2 large eggs
1¼ cups whole milk
½ cup vegetable oil
2 teaspoons pure vanilla extract
1 cup hot coffee

FOR THE CHOCOLATE FROSTING

1 cup heavy cream
2 cups best-quality dark chocolate
¼ teaspoon fine sea salt

DECORATING INGREDIENTS AND TOOLS

2 large baking sheets
Piping bag fitted with a large open circle tip
9-by-13-inch cake pan
Cake board or cake platter
Candy thermometer

TO MAKE THE MERINGUE BONES: Ensure that the metal bowl of your stand mixer is completely grease-free by wiping it with a halved lemon, then rinse and dry it thoroughly.

In the bowl of a stand mixer fitted with the whisk attachment or a large bowl with a handheld mixer, mix the egg whites and sugar on low speed to combine into a sugar slurry. Fill a medium saucepan with a few inches of water and place it on the stove over medium-high heat. Set the mixer bowl on top of the saucepan to create a double boiler, making sure the mixer bowl doesn't touch the water.

Heat the egg and sugar mixture until it reaches 160°F on a thermometer, whisking occasionally, 5 to 7 minutes.

Carefully return the mixing bowl to the stand mixer with the whisk attachment in place. Bring the mixer up to high speed and beat the mixture for 8 to 10 minutes, until you've reached stiff peaks. Add the vanilla extract and whip to combine, about 15 seconds.

Preheat the oven to 200°F.

Line two large baking sheets with parchment paper. Fill the piping bag fitted with a large open circle tip with the meringue. Pipe bone shapes, about 4 to 5 inches long, in one continuous motion—pipe an "S" shape, then continue piping out the long part of the bone, with an "S" shape on the other end.

Bake until crisp, 1 to 1½ hours, being careful they don't brown. Turn the oven off completely and allow the meringue bones to dry out overnight in the oven.

TO MAKE THE CHOCOLATE CAKE: Preheat the oven to 350°F. Generously spray the entire cake pan with cooking spray or vegetable oil, then line the bottom with parchment paper cut to size. Spritz the parchment paper and set aside.

In the bowl of a stand mixer fitted with the paddle attachment or a large bowl with a handheld mixer, combine on low speed the flour, cocoa powder, sugar, baking soda, baking powder, and salt.

Add the eggs, milk, vegetable oil, vanilla, and coffee. Beat on low speed until combined and smooth, about 2 minutes, scraping down the sides of the bowl as needed.

Pour into the prepared cake pan and bake for 30 to 35 minutes, until the top of the cake is springy and a toothpick inserted into the center of the cake comes out with only moist crumbs. Let cool completely.

CONTINUES ON PAGE 92

TO MAKE THE FROSTING: In a medium saucepan, heat the cream on low heat until it reaches a low bubbling boil, being careful not to burn it. Remove the saucepan from the heat. Add the chocolate, swirling the pan to cover the chocolate completely. Allow to sit for 10 minutes. Carefully whisk together to form a glossy ganache. Power-chill the ganache in the fridge for 30 to 45 minutes, until firmer but not solidified. Add the ganache to the bowl of a stand mixer fitted with the paddle attachment or a large bowl with a handheld mixer. Beat on medium speed until lightened in color and volumized. Add the ¼ teaspoon of fine sea salt. Beat on high speed for another minute to volumize further.

TO ASSEMBLE THE CAKE: Turn the cake out onto a cake board or cake platter. Frost the entire cake with the whipped ganache, using thick swoops to decorate the top of the cake. Add the meringue bones in an artful and even array, and serve!

Vampire's Coffin Blackberry Cake

The Vampire Brothers' coffins creak open into the dark of Halloween Town, and they're ready to help out with Jack Skellington's Halloween-inspired Christmas! After a long night of painting creepy yellow duck toys, back into their funerary boxes they go for a light rest. This vampire coffin–inspired cake gets a buttercream piping upgrade and a delicious blackberry-laced filling.

Yield: 1 cake, 15 to 20 servings | Skill Level: Easy

FOR THE BLACKBERRY JAM CAKE

3 cups cake flour

1 tablespoon baking powder

1 teaspoon fine sea salt

1 cup unsalted butter, room temperature

1½ cups granulated sugar

4 large eggs

1 tablespoon pure vanilla extract

1¼ cups whole milk

¼ cup blackberry jam

1 cup blackberries, chopped

FOR THE VANILLA BUTTERCREAM

1 cup unsalted butter, room temperature

2 cups icing sugar, sifted

1 teaspoon pure vanilla extract

Pinch of salt

FOR THE CHOCOLATE SWISS MERINGUE BUTTERCREAM

½ lemon

1 cup egg whites (about 8 large egg whites)

2¼ cups granulated sugar

2¼ cups unsalted butter, room temperature

2 teaspoons pure vanilla extract

Pinch of fine sea salt

¼ cup best-quality chocolate, melted and cooled

DECORATING INGREDIENTS AND TOOLS

9-by-13-inch cake pan

Cake board or cake platter

Sharp knife

Cake bench scraper or offset spatula

Gel food coloring in two colors, such as fuchsia pink and violet

Piping bags fitted with various open star tips

Bat candies or sprinkles (optional)

Edible flowers and blackberries (optional)

Candy thermometer

TO MAKE THE CAKE: Preheat the oven to 350°F. Generously spray the entire cake pan with cooking spray or vegetable oil, then line the bottom with parchment paper cut to size. Spritz the parchment paper and set aside.

In a large bowl, whisk together the cake flour, baking powder, and salt and set aside.

In the bowl of a stand mixer fitted with the paddle attachment or a large bowl with a handheld mixer, beat the butter and sugar on high speed until light, fluffy, and doubled in volume, about 2 minutes, scraping down the sides of the bowl as needed.

With the mixer on low speed, add the eggs one at a time, mixing each time until incorporated. Add the vanilla extract and mix on low speed to combine.

Add the flour mixture in three additions, alternating with the milk, beginning and ending with the flour mixture until a smooth batter forms, about 1 minute.

Fold in the blackberry jam and chopped blackberries.

Pour the batter into the prepared cake pan and bake for 35 to 40 minutes, until lightly golden brown and a toothpick inserted into the center of the cake comes out with only moist crumbs. Let cool completely before the next step.

TO MAKE THE VANILLA BUTTERCREAM: In the bowl of a stand mixer fitted with the paddle attachment or a large bowl with a handheld mixer, beat the butter, icing sugar, vanilla extract, and salt on low speed to combine. Increase to high speed and beat until light, fluffy, and doubled in volume, about 2 minutes.

TO MAKE THE CHOCOLATE SWISS MERINGUE BUTTERCREAM: Ensure that the metal bowl of your stand mixer is completely grease-free by wiping it with a halved lemon, then rinse and dry it thoroughly.

In the bowl of a stand mixer fitted with the whisk attachment or a large bowl with a handheld mixer, mix the egg whites and sugar on low speed to combine into a sugar slurry. Fill a medium saucepan with a few inches of water and place it on the stove over medium-high heat. Set the mixer bowl on top of the saucepan to create a double boiler, making sure the mixer bowl doesn't touch the water.

Heat the egg and sugar mixture until it reaches 160°F on a thermometer, whisking occasionally, 5 to 7 minutes.

Carefully return the mixing bowl to the stand mixer, with the whisk attachment in place. Bring the mixer up to high speed and beat the mixture for 8 to 10 minutes, until you've reached stiff peaks.

Swap out the whisk for the paddle attachment. Make sure your meringue has cooled sufficiently enough so that when you add the butter it won't completely

CONTINUES ON PAGE 95

melt away. The bowl should be only slightly warm at this point.

With the mixer on low speed, add the butter a few pieces at a time, until all the butter is incorporated—it will look like thick soup at this point. Add the vanilla extract and salt.

Bring the mixer speed up to medium-high and beat until a fluffy meringue buttercream forms, 2 to 3 minutes. Add the cooled chocolate and beat for another 30 seconds to incorporate.

TO ASSEMBLE THE CAKE: Turn the cooled cake out onto a cake board or cake platter. Using a sharp knife, trim the cake judiciously into a coffin shape. Trim the top of the cake to make it level.

Spread a thin layer of blackberry jam on the top of the cake.

Frost a thin crumb coat layer of chocolate buttercream over the entire cake, reserving some of the buttercream for the second coat and for piping the borders, and refrigerate for 15 minutes to set.

Frost a second coat of chocolate buttercream, using a cake bench scraper or offset spatula to smooth.

Divide the vanilla buttercream and tint it in two different colors—fuchsia pink and dark violet, for example.

Fill a piping bag fitted with a small open star tip with the reserved chocolate buttercream. Pipe the bottom border of the coffin cake, and pipe the outline of the coffin on the top of the cake. Using other piping bags fitted with other tips, embellish the coffin with the colored vanilla buttercream, making drop stars and mini rosettes. Pipe "RIP" on the coffin, and decorate further with bone or bat candy sprinkles, fresh blackberries, and edible flowers, if desired.

Marshmallow Spider Web Mocha Cake

Get tangled up in this sticky-sweet marshmallow spider web–covered mocha chocolate cake. It's adorned with a few skittering spiders that would be *very* at home as the fashionable brooch on the Mayor of Halloween Town's coat, as the two-faced politician both panics from nerves and praises with glee!

Yield: 1 cake, 15 to 20 servings | Skill Level: Easy

FOR THE MOCHA CAKE

¾ cup hot coffee

¾ cup Dutch-process cocoa powder

¾ cup sour cream

3 cups cake flour

1 teaspoon baking soda

1 teaspoon fine sea salt

1½ cups unsalted butter, room temperature

2¼ cups granulated sugar

4 large eggs

1 tablespoon pure coffee extract

1 teaspoon pure vanilla extract

FOR THE COFFEE MILK SOAK

1 cup whole milk

1 teaspoon instant espresso powder

4 tablespoons granulated sugar

FOR THE MOCHA BUTTERCREAM

2 cups unsalted butter, room temperature

2½ cups icing sugar, sifted

2 teaspoons pure coffee extract

1 teaspoon pure vanilla extract

1½ cups best-quality bittersweet or dark chocolate, melted and cooled to room temperature

DECORATING INGREDIENTS AND TOOLS

9-by-13-inch cake pan

Black fondant

Cake board

Serrated knife

Small offset spatula

16 large marshmallows

TO MAKE THE CAKE: Preheat the oven to 350°F. Generously spray the entire cake pan with cooking spray or vegetable oil, then line the bottom with parchment paper cut to size. Spritz the parchment paper and set aside.

In a medium bowl, whisk the hot coffee with the cocoa powder until smooth. Whisk in the sour cream and let cool.

In a medium bowl, whisk together the cake flour, baking soda, and salt and set aside.

In the bowl of a stand mixer fitted with the paddle attachment or a large bowl with a handheld mixer, beat the butter and sugar on high speed until light, fluffy, and doubled in volume, about 2 minutes, scraping down the sides of the bowl as needed. With the mixer on low speed, add the eggs one at a time, until incorporated. Add the coffee extract and vanilla extract and mix to combine.

With the mixture on low speed, add the flour mixture in two parts, alternating with the cocoa mixture and beginning and ending with the flour mixture. Beat until combined and a smooth batter forms, about 1 minute.

Pour the batter into the prepared cake pan and bake for 35 to 40 minutes, until the cake is springy to the touch and a toothpick inserted into the center comes out with only moist crumbs. Let cool completely on a wire rack.

TO MAKE THE COFFEE MILK SOAK: In a small saucepan over medium heat, whisk together the milk, espresso powder, and sugar, whisking constantly until dissolved and combined. Remove and let cool completely.

TO MAKE THE MOCHA BUTTERCREAM: In the bowl of a stand mixer fitted with the paddle attachment or a large bowl with a handheld mixer, beat the butter, icing sugar, coffee extract, and vanilla extract on low speed to combine, then increase to high speed and beat until light, fluffy, and doubled in volume, about 2 minutes, scraping down the sides of the bowl as needed. With the mixer on low speed, add the melted and cooled chocolate, and mix until combined and smooth.

TO ASSEMBLE THE CAKE: Using clean dry hands, mold the black spiders out of fondant. Make one black marble-size ball for the body, and attach a smaller ball for the head. Roll out thin log-like pieces with pointed ends for the legs, and attach the pieces to the body using tiny amounts of water to stick. Place on parchment paper and allow to dry and adhere completely. Make them in various sizes! You can make as many as you like.

Turn the completely cooled cake out onto a cake board and trim and level the cake using a serrated knife. Using a pastry brush or teaspoon, add a generous amount of coffee milk soak to the cake, allowing it to soak in before adding more, being careful not to soak the cake to mush. Frost a thin layer of mocha buttercream over the entire cake. Refrigerate for 20 minutes to set the buttercream, then frost a second layer of buttercream, either keeping it smooth or creating swoops in the frosting using a small offset spatula. Refrigerate the cake for 20 minutes while you prepare the marshmallows.

In a medium saucepan or in the microwave, melt the marshmallows until they've lost their shape and are deflated and melty. Wearing food-safe gloves, pull the marshmallow mixture to stretch until thin and web-like. Pull the stretched webbing all across and over the sheet cake to mimic spider webs. Once cooled completely and firmed up, add the black fondant spiders in an artful pattern to the top of the cake.

Pink Easter Bunny Cut-Up Cake

When Lock, Shock, and Barrel are sent to kidnap Sandy Claws, they accidentally come back with a confused pink Easter Bunny instead—who gets the fright of its furry pink life when it hops over to the shuddersome, corpse-pale Behemoth! This retro pink bunny cake will add some bright color and shock-faced cottontail fun to your *The Nightmare Before Christmas* party!

Yield: 1 cake, 15 to 20 servings | Skill Level: Easy

FOR THE COCONUT CAKE

3 cups cake flour

1 tablespoon baking powder

1 teaspoon fine sea salt

1 cup shredded coconut

1 cup unsalted butter, room temperature

1½ cups granulated sugar

4 large eggs, room temperature

1 teaspoon pure coconut extract

1 tablespoon pure vanilla extract

1½ cups full-fat coconut cream

FOR THE COCONUT BUTTERCREAM

2 cups unsalted butter, room temperature

4 cups icing sugar, sifted

1 teaspoon pure vanilla extract

1 teaspoon pure coconut extract

Pinch of salt

DECORATING INGREDIENTS AND TOOLS

Two 8-by-2-inch round cake pans

Sharp knife

Cake board or platter

Green and pink gel food coloring

One 14-ounce bag of shredded white coconut

1 large resealable plastic bag

Piping bag fitted with a small open star tip

White fondant

Small circle-shaped cookie cutter or circular bottom edge of a large piping tip

Paring knife

Bottom edge of a small piping tip

Small amount of black fondant

TO MAKE THE CAKE: Preheat the oven to 350°F. Generously spray both cake pans with cooking spray or vegetable oil, then line the bottoms with parchment paper cut to size. Spritz the parchment paper and set aside.

In a large bowl, whisk together the cake flour, baking powder, salt, and shredded coconut and set aside.

In the bowl of a stand mixer fitted with the paddle attachment or a large bowl with a handheld mixer, beat the butter and sugar on high speed until light, fluffy, and doubled in volume, about 2 minutes, scraping down the sides of the bowl as needed.

With the mixer on low speed, add the eggs one at a time, mixing each time until incorporated. Add the coconut extract and vanilla extract and mix on low speed to combine.

Add the flour mixture in three additions, alternating with the coconut cream, beginning and ending with the flour mixture until a smooth batter forms, about 1 minute.

Divide the batter evenly between the cake pans and bake for 25 to 30 minutes, until the cake is lightly golden, slightly domed, and a toothpick inserted into the center comes back with only moist crumbs. Let cool completely on wire racks.

TO MAKE THE BUTTERCREAM: In the bowl of a stand mixer fitted with the paddle attachment or a large bowl with a handheld mixer, beat the butter, icing sugar, vanilla extract, coconut extract, and salt on low speed to combine. Increase to high speed and beat until light, fluffy, and doubled in volume, about 2 minutes.

TO ASSEMBLE THE CAKE: Using a sharp knife, cut one of the cooled cake rounds into three pieces—two stretched football-like shapes cut from either side of the cake for bunny ears, leaving a bow-tie shape. On a cake board or cake platter, assemble the pieces in a bird's-eye view: one round cake, two ears on top of the round cake, and a bow tie nestled into the bottom of the cake.

Divide the buttercream. Reserve 1½ cups and tint it a light green. Color the rest of the buttercream using the pink gel color.

Prepare the coconut: In a large resealable plastic bag, add the shredded white coconut and a tiny drop of pink gel food coloring. Zip the bag, and then using your fingers,

CONTINUES ON PAGE 100

massage the coconut shreds around with the pink gel color until the coconut is colored pink. Use more gel color if needed, but avoid using too much in order to keep the coconut shreds dry.

Frost the entire round cake and two ear pieces with a generous amount of pink buttercream. Wearing food-safe gloves, pat the pink coconut shreds against the buttercream-frosted round cake, pressing the coconut shreds into the buttercream. Repeat with the bunny ears.

Frost a thin coat of green buttercream on the bow tie. Fill the piping bag fitted with the open star tip with the remaining green buttercream. Pipe the entire bow tie with little green drop stars.

Roll out the white fondant to ¼ inch thick. Make stunned bunny eyes by using a 1- to 2-inch round small cookie cutter or the bottom edge of a large piping tip to cut out two circles of the white fondant. Punch out one more white circle for the bow tie center, if desired. Roll out the black fondant and, using the bottom edge of a small piping tip, punch out two smaller circles. Adhere the black irises to the eye whites using a tiny dab of water. Roll some black fondant in clean hands and make a little bunny nose. Roll some long thin log-like pieces for bunny whiskers.

Using a paring knife, cut out two bunny buck teeth from the white fondant.

Place the facial features onto the bunny by gently pressing into the cake! Place the white fondant bow tie center onto the bow tie.

The One Hiding Under Your Bed Brownie Cake

In the opening song "This Is Halloween," we meet all the horrific creatures concealed in the dark corners of our homes—including The One Hiding Under Your Bed, with its glaring, blood-colored eyes and razor fangs ready to snap at your ankles. Your sharp teeth will be happy to bite into this rich, delicious brownie cake decorated after your favorite under-the-bed ghoul!

Yield: 1 brownie cake, 12 servings | Skill Level: Easy

FOR THE BROWNIE CAKE

Cocoa powder for dusting (optional)

⅔ cup unsalted butter

¾ cup best-quality semisweet or dark chocolate

2 teaspoons pure vanilla extract

4 large eggs

¾ teaspoon fine sea salt

2 cups granulated sugar

1 cup all-purpose flour

FOR THE CHOCOLATE GLAZE

¼ cup unsalted butter

3 to 4 tablespoons whole milk

¾ cup best-quality semisweet or dark chocolate

1 cup icing sugar, sifted, plus more if needed

Pinch of salt

DECORATING INGREDIENTS AND TOOLS

9-inch square cake pan

Cake board or cake platter

Sharp paring knife or kitchen scissors

1 large bright red strawberry or red fruit leather

Toasted slivered almonds

TO MAKE THE BROWNIE CAKE: Preheat the oven to 350°F. Generously spray the entire cake pan with cooking spray or vegetable oil, then line the bottom with parchment paper cut to size. Spritz the parchment paper and lightly dust with flour or cocoa powder.

In a small saucepan over low heat, melt the butter and chocolate together, stirring until smooth and glossy. Remove from heat and stir in the vanilla extract.

In the bowl of a stand mixer fitted with the paddle attachment or a large bowl with a handheld mixer, beat the eggs and salt together. Add the sugar and beat on high speed until lightened in color, 8 to 10 minutes. With the mixer on low speed, add the chocolate mixture to the egg mixture until just combined. With the mixer on low speed, add the flour and mix until just incorporated.

Pour the brownie batter into the prepared pan and bake for 40 to 45 minutes, until the brownie cake is fudgy, set, and a toothpick inserted into the center comes out with not-quite-but-almost-baked batter/moist crumbs.

Cool completely on a wire rack.

TO MAKE THE GLAZE: In a small saucepan, melt together the butter, 3 tablespoons of the milk, and chocolate, blending until smooth. Add icing sugar and salt and mix until incorporated and smooth. If the mixture is too thin, add additional icing sugar 1 tablespoon at a time, keeping in mind that it will add sweetness. If the glaze is too thick, add the remaining tablespoon of milk.

TO ASSEMBLE THE CAKE: Carefully turn out the brownie cake onto a cake board or cake platter. Pour the thickened and cooled glaze onto the cooled cake and let set for 30 minutes.

Using a sharp paring knife, cut the large strawberry in half, cutting each half into the shape of a large almond-shaped evil red eye. Alternately, use kitchen scissors to cut out large red almond-shaped eyes from red fruit leather.

Place onto the cake, adding slivered almonds for sharp teeth!

Chapter 5

Showstopping Spectacle Cakes

Slithery Gift-Gobbling Snake Bundt Cake

Santa Jack lets loose a reptilian holiday gift for one lucky family—the orange and black striped snake, which gulps down the family's Christmas gifts and the tinsel tree, too! Delight your guests with a black and orange striped chocolate sour cream cake, cleverly crafted from one Bundt cake. If you want to serve many guests and you have space on your dessert table, you could always try making a twice-as-large snake cake by doubling the recipe and putting four cut Bundt pieces together to make a longer snake! Note: This cake uses a lot of orange and brown candies, so make sure you have enough.

Yield: 1 cake, 18 to 20 servings | Skill Level: Easy

FOR THE CAKE

2¼ cups all-purpose flour

¾ cup cocoa powder

1 teaspoon baking soda

1 teaspoon salt

½ cup whole milk

½ cup full-fat sour cream

1 cup unsalted butter, plus more to grease the pan

1½ cups granulated sugar

4 large eggs

2 teaspoons pure vanilla extract

FOR THE BUTTERCREAM

2 cups unsalted butter

4 cups icing sugar, sifted

2 teaspoons pure vanilla extract

Pinch of salt

½ teaspoon orange gel food coloring

DECORATING INGREDIENTS AND TOOLS

10-inch Bundt cake pan

Wooden skewer

Large platter or cake board

Paring knife

Offset spatula

Candy-coated chocolate in orange and dark brown

2 large sugar pearls or white chocolate chips

Mini chocolate chips or edible marker

Red licorice

Cake platter or cake board

TO MAKE THE CAKE: Preheat the oven to 350°F. Generously spray the entire cake pan with cooking spray or vegetable oil.

In a large bowl, whisk together the all-purpose flour, cocoa powder, baking soda, and salt.

In a medium bowl, mix to combine the whole milk and sour cream.

In the bowl of a stand mixer fitted with the paddle attachment or a large bowl with a handheld mixer, beat the butter and sugar on high speed until light and fluffy, 2 to 4 minutes. Add the eggs and beat on low speed to combine. Add the vanilla extract. On low speed, add half of the flour mixture, then half of the milk mixture, alternating between the two until they're just combined.

Pour the cake batter into the prepared Bundt pan and bake for 55 to 60 minutes, until a wooden skewer inserted into the cake comes out with only moist crumbs. Cool the cake completely on a wire rack before reusing the Bundt pan for the optional second cake.

TO MAKE THE BUTTERCREAM: In a stand mixer fitted with the paddle attachment or a large bowl with a handheld mixer, beat the butter on high speed until light and fluffy, about 2 minutes. Scrape down the sides of the bowl and add the icing sugar, vanilla, salt, and orange gel color. Cover the mixer with a damp towel to avoid an icing sugar dust storm. Pulse on low speed to combine the ingredients; once combined, beat on high speed for 2 minutes, until doubled in volume.

TO ASSEMBLE THE CAKE: For easier assembly, make sure that your Bundt cake is completely cooled. With a sharp knife, slice the cake in half vertically. Add a little buttercream to the large platter or cake board and place the Bundt cake pieces to form one "S" shape. Using a paring knife, trim the head of the cake into a triangular shape and the tail of the cake into a thin, triangular tail-like shape (you can save the cake scraps for snacking on later!).

Using an offset spatula, frost the entire cake with the orange buttercream. If it can fit in the fridge, chill the cake for 15 minutes before frosting with a second layer of buttercream.

Using orange and dark brown coated chocolate candies, decorate the slithery snake with thick stripes. Finish the cake with two snake eyes by adhering two chocolate chip irises to two white candy pearls with a tiny dot of buttercream or dots of black edible marker ink for the irises and nostrils. Cut a small piece of red licorice into a tongue shape and place it in the snake's mouth with buttercream. Merry Chrisssssthmas!!!

Holiday Door to Christmas Town Cake

Jack Skellington has many choices when he reaches the intriguing Holiday Doors in the forest—the magical tree doorways to all the various holiday worlds! When he opens the Christmas Door, he tumbles down into a world so unlike his own that he becomes obsessed with Christmas! In this inspired cake, buttercream chocolate bark and a piped Christmas tree give the illusion of the Holiday Door to Christmas Town! Note: You can make the cake in four 6-by-2-inch round cake pans, three 7-by-2-inch round cake pans, or even three 8-by-2-inch round cake pans, but the cake won't be as tall and door-like!

Yield: 1 cake, 12 to 16 servings | Skill Level: Easy

FOR THE CHOCOLATE GINGERBREAD CAKE

1½ cups all-purpose flour
1 cup granulated sugar
½ cup light brown sugar
¾ cup Dutch-process cocoa powder
1½ teaspoons baking soda
1 teaspoon baking powder
1 teaspoon ground cinnamon
1 teaspoon ground ginger
½ teaspoon ground nutmeg
1 teaspoon fine sea salt
¼ cup vegetable oil
¾ cup buttermilk
2 large eggs, room temperature

1 teaspoon vanilla
¼ cup molasses
¾ cup hot coffee

FOR THE VANILLA BUTTERCREAM

1 cup unsalted butter, room temperature
2 cups icing sugar, sifted
1 teaspoon pure vanilla extract
Pinch of salt

FOR THE CHOCOLATE BUTTERCREAM

2 cups unsalted butter, room temperature
3 cups icing sugar, sifted
½ cup Dutch-process cocoa powder
2 teaspoons pure vanilla extract
Pinch of salt

DECORATING INGREDIENTS AND TOOLS

Four 6-by-2-inch round cake pans
Cake board or plate
Serrated knife
Small offset spatula
2 piping bags fitted with open star tips
Toothpick or chopstick
Yellow and green gel food coloring
1 piping bag fitted with a small open circle tip
Various colored candies and candy cane pieces
Scissors
Yellow craft paper
Tape
Wooden skewer, cut in half

TO MAKE THE CAKE: Preheat the oven to 350°F. Generously spray all cake pans with nonstick cooking spray and line each with parchment paper cut to size, then spritz again.

In the bowl of a stand mixer fitted with the paddle attachment or a large bowl with a handheld mixer, mix together on low speed the flour, granulated sugar, brown sugar, cocoa powder, baking soda, baking powder, cinnamon, ginger, nutmeg, and salt to combine.

In a medium bowl, whisk to combine the vegetable oil, buttermilk, eggs, vanilla, and molasses.

With the mixer on low speed, carefully add the oil mixture to the flour mixture. Stream in the hot coffee to combine. Mix until combined and a smooth batter forms, about 30 seconds.

Divide the batter evenly among the prepared cake pans. Bake for 20 to 24 minutes, until the cake springs back to the touch and a toothpick inserted in the center comes out with only moist crumbs.

Cool cakes completely before decorating.

TO MAKE THE VANILLA BUTTERCREAM: In the bowl of a stand mixer fitted with the paddle attachment or a large bowl with a handheld mixer, beat the butter, icing sugar, vanilla extract, and salt on low speed to combine. Increase to high speed and beat until light, fluffy, and doubled in volume, about 2 minutes.

TO MAKE THE CHOCOLATE BUTTERCREAM: In the bowl of a stand mixer fitted with the paddle attachment or a large bowl with a handheld mixer, beat the butter, icing sugar, cocoa powder, vanilla extract, and salt on low speed to combine. Increase to high speed and beat until light, fluffy, and doubled in volume, about 2 minutes.

TO ASSEMBLE THE CAKE: Have a cake board or plate ready. Add a dollop of vanilla buttercream to the center to adhere the first layer. Place the first cooled cake layer flat side down on the cake board. Trim the cake layer with a serrated knife to level it. Add a generous amount of chocolate buttercream to the center and spread to the edges using a small offset spatula. Take the next cake layer and trim to level. Place on top of the first frosted layer. Frost the second layer. For the last cake layer, trim it to level, then place cut side down, so you have a flat and level top of the cake.

Frost the entire cake with a thin layer of chocolate buttercream, then refrigerate for 20 minutes to set the buttercream.

Remove the cake from the fridge. Frost just the top of the cake with a layer of chocolate buttercream; use your offset spatula to create concentric circles on the top of the cake, like a tree stump. Fill one of the piping bags fitted with an open star tip with the remaining chocolate buttercream and, starting from the bottom of the cake and working your way upward, pipe straight lines of buttercream all the way around the cake. Using a toothpick or chopstick, draw into the buttercream on the side of the cake the outline of a large Christmas tree. Use your offset spatula to carefully remove the buttercream just from inside this tree shape; smooth with an offset spatula to prepare the area.

Divide the vanilla buttercream. Add ¼ cup vanilla buttercream to a small bowl, and tint it with ½ teaspoon of yellow gel color. Color the rest of the buttercream with ½ teaspoon of green gel color. Add the green buttercream to the piping bag fitted with the second open star tip. Pipe the outline of the Christmas tree. Add vertical lines of piping to fill the entire tree. Fill the piping bag fitted with the small open circle tip with yellow buttercream; pipe yellow garlands zigzagging across the tree. Add bright colored candies for Christmas tree baubles, with one distinct bauble as the door handle. Cut out a star from the yellow craft paper; tape it to the wooden skewer and insert into the cake for the top of the tree.

Pumpkin Head Tres Leches Cake

Double the pumpkin fun with this *gourd*-geous "This is Halloween" sweet milk-soaked pumpkin spice Bundt cake. It's fashioned to look like one of the jack-o'-lanterns perched on the hill of Halloween Town's Pumpkin Field. It's a scrumptious pumpkin patch party win-win! Note: This recipe makes two Bundt cakes, to be stacked on top of each other to form a 3D pumpkin.

Yield: 1 cake, 18 to 24 servings | Skill Level: Moderate

FOR THE PUMPKIN SPICE BUNDT CAKES

4½ cups granulated sugar

2 cups vegetable oil

6 large eggs

6 cups all-purpose flour

4 teaspoons baking soda

2 teaspoons ground cinnamon

2 teaspoons ground ginger

2 teaspoons nutmeg

2 teaspoons fine sea salt

Two 15-ounce cans pumpkin puree

FOR THE TRES LECHES CAKE SOAK

3 cups evaporated milk

3 cups sweetened condensed milk

1 cup half-and-half cream

FOR THE TRES LECHES BUTTERCREAM

3 cups unsalted butter, room temperature

6 cups icing sugar

2 teaspoons pure vanilla extract

½ cup tres leches cake soak

Pinch of salt

DECORATING INGREDIENTS AND TOOLS

Two 10-inch Bundt cake pans

Orange gel food coloring

Knife

Cake board or plate

Small offset spatula

Black fondant

Paring knife

TO MAKE THE BUNDT CAKES: Preheat the oven to 350°F. Spray the Bundt cake pans with nonstick cooking spray and lightly flour.

In the bowl of a stand mixer fitted with the paddle attachment or a large bowl with a handheld mixer, beat the sugar and vegetable oil on high speed until light and fluffy, about 2 minutes. With the mixer on low speed, add the eggs, one at a time, beating well after each addition.

In a medium bowl, whisk together the flour, baking soda, cinnamon, ginger, nutmeg, and salt.

With the mixer on low speed, add the flour mixture to the oil mixture in three additions, alternating with the pumpkin puree, beginning and ending with the flour mixture, until a smooth batter forms, about 1 minute total.

Split the batter evenly between the prepared Bundt cake pans and bake for 55 to 60 minutes, until a toothpick inserted into the center comes out with only moist crumbs. Cool for 15 minutes in the pans, then invert onto a wire rack to cool completely.

TO MAKE THE TRES LECHES CAKE SOAK: In a medium bowl, whisk together the evaporated milk, sweetened condensed milk, and half-and-half cream. Reserve ½ cup for the buttercream.

TO MAKE THE BUTTERCREAM: In the bowl of a stand mixer fitted with the paddle attachment or a large bowl with a handheld mixer, beat the butter, icing sugar, vanilla, reserved ½ cup of tres leches cake soak, and salt on low speed to incorporate. Increase to high speed and beat until light, fluffy, and doubled in volume, about 2 minutes, scraping down the sides of the bowl as needed. Add 3 to 4 teaspoons of orange gel color to tint the buttercream.

CONTINUES ON PAGE 110

TO ASSEMBLE THE CAKE: Gather the two completely cooled Bundt cakes. Turn the cakes upside down and trim 1 inch off the bottoms of the cakes to level them, and so that the cake soak can soak into them. Save the trimmings for decoration usage later.

Place some buttercream onto a cake board or plate, then place the first cake upside down onto the cake board, adhering to the buttercream. Using a pastry brush or teaspoon, add a generous amount of cake soak to the exposed cake. Add a generous amount of buttercream to frost the first layer.

With the second cake also upside down, add a generous amount of cake soak and allow it to soak in before inverting the layer on top of the buttercream-frosted first layer. Press the cake gently down to adhere.

Stuff some of the trimmings into the center Bundt cake hole to fill it up, alternating with dollops of buttercream.

Frost the entire cake with a first layer of buttercream, using an offset spatula to smooth and define the Bundt cake "pumpkin" ridges. Refrigerate until firm, about 20 minutes. Remove from the refrigerator and do a second and final, smooth coat of buttercream, smoothing and shaping it into a pumpkin.

Mix up the remaining trimmings with buttercream to make a cake pop–like "stem" shape. Roll it into a large stem shape and refrigerate until firm. Cover with black fondant, and place into the top of the cake. If you used up all the trimmings, don't fret—simply mold the shape of a stem from the black fondant. Use a paring knife or fork to carefully make textural lines in the stem.

Use a paring knife to cut out jack-o'-lantern eyes, nose, and sharp jagged teeth from the black fondant and press into the cake.

Swinging Skeleton Skull Peanut Butter Cake

Transform a skull cake pan into one of the swinging skeleton skulls! The Skeleton Tree is a citizen of Halloween Town, a large towering timber walking around with skeletons swinging from its bare branches. This delicious peanut butter cake is tinged slime-green for extra creepy fun, with black frosted hollow eyes, nose, and mouth, eliciting some eerie vibes for your treats table.

Yield: 1 cake, 12 to 16 servings | Skill Level: Easy

FOR THE PEANUT BUTTER CAKE

2 cups all-purpose flour

1 teaspoon fine sea salt

1 teaspoon baking soda

1 cup creamy peanut butter

½ cup unsalted butter

1 cup granulated sugar

1 cup brown sugar

2 eggs, room temperature

½ cup buttermilk

1 teaspoon pure vanilla extract

FOR THE VANILLA BUTTERCREAM

1½ cups unsalted butter, room temperature

3 cups icing sugar

1 teaspoon pure vanilla extract

Pinch of salt

DECORATING INGREDIENTS AND TOOLS

1 Wilton skull cake pan

Cupcake pan and paper liners

Black and neon green gel food coloring

TO MAKE THE CAKE: Preheat the oven to 350°F. Spray the skull pan with nonstick cooking spray and set aside. Prepare an additional cupcake tin lined with paper liners for any leftover cake batter.

In a medium bowl, whisk together the flour, salt, and baking soda.

In the bowl of a stand mixer fitted with the paddle attachment or a large bowl with a handheld mixer, mix together the peanut butter, butter, granulated sugar, and brown sugar on low speed to combine.

With the mixer on low speed, add the eggs, buttermilk, and vanilla to the bowl and mix to incorporate.

With the mixer on low speed, add the flour mixture and mix until incorporated and a smooth batter forms, about 1 minute, scraping down the sides of the bowl as needed.

Pour the batter into the prepared skull cake pan, about ⅔ full. Divide any remaining batter evenly in prepared cupcake pan.

Bake the cupcakes for 16 to 18 minutes and the cake for 20 to 24 minutes, until cake springs back to the touch, is lightly golden, and a toothpick inserted into the center comes out with only moist crumbs. Let cool in pan for 15 minutes, then let cool completely on wire rack.

TO MAKE THE BUTTERCREAM: In the bowl of a stand mixer fitted with the paddle attachment or a large bowl with a handheld mixer, beat the butter, icing sugar, vanilla extract, and salt on low speed to combine. Increase to high speed and beat until light, fluffy, and doubled in volume, about 2 minutes.

TO ASSEMBLE THE CAKE: Divide the buttercream: Place ½ cup buttercream in a small bowl and tint it black using the black gel coloring. Tint the rest of it a slime-neon green.

Frost the entire cake with the green buttercream. Refrigerate for 20 minutes, until firm. Remove from the fridge and frost the eyes, nose, and mouth cavities with the black buttercream.

Black Cat Banana Cake

In the shadows of Halloween Town lurk slinky black cats, getting into mischief. Meow's the time to tuck into this *cat*-tabulous banana chocolate cake! Frosted with black chocolate ganache and feline yellow eyes, this kitty might very well snuggle up to Sally if it's feeling friendly.

Yield: 1 cake, 12 to 16 servings | Skill Level: Easy

FOR THE BANANA CHOCOLATE CHIP CAKE

2¼ cups cake flour

¾ teaspoon baking soda

¾ teaspoon fine sea salt

1 cup mashed ripe bananas (2 large bananas)

½ cup buttermilk

1 tablespoon pure vanilla extract

1 cup unsalted butter, room temperature

1⅓ cups granulated sugar

2 large eggs, room temperature

1 cup best-quality dark or bittersweet chocolate chips

FOR THE CHOCOLATE GANACHE

3 cups heavy cream

3 cups best-quality dark or bittersweet chocolate, chopped

Pinch of salt

2 teaspoons black gel color, plus more as needed

DECORATING INGREDIENTS AND TOOLS

Three 7-by-2-inch round cake pans

Black fondant

Wooden skewers

Yellow and pink fondant (or a pink candy)

Paring knife

White fondant (optional)

TO MAKE THE CAKE: Preheat the oven to 350°F.

Spray the cake pans with nonstick cooking spray and line with parchment paper circles cut to size. Spray the parchment paper and set aside.

In a medium bowl, whisk to combine the cake flour, baking soda, and salt.

In a medium bowl, mix together the bananas, buttermilk, and vanilla extract.

In the bowl of a stand mixer fitted with the paddle attachment or a large bowl with a handheld mixer, beat together the butter and sugar until light and fluffy, about 2 minutes. With the mixer on low speed, add the eggs one at a time, beating to incorporate after each addition.

With the mixer on low speed, add the flour mixture in three portions, alternating with the banana buttermilk mixture, beginning and ending with the flour mixture, until just mixed, about 30 seconds. Use a rubber spatula to fold it a few times if needed. Gently fold in the chocolate chips.

Divide the batter evenly into the prepared cake pans and bake for 22 to 25 minutes, until cake is lightly browned and a toothpick inserted into the center comes out with only moist crumbs. Let cool completely on wire racks.

TO MAKE THE GANACHE: In a medium saucepan set over low heat, heat the cream to a low boil, being careful not to burn it. Remove from heat and add the chocolate, swirling the pan to cover the chocolate completely. Allow to sit for 10 minutes. Carefully whisk together to form a ganache. Add the pinch of salt and black gel color, whisking to combine. Add more black as needed to develop a deeper color, if desired. Cool in fridge to quicken the cooling, if desired. Allow it to thicken to frosting consistency—be careful not to leave it refrigerated for too long, as it will solidify!

TO ASSEMBLE THE CAKE: Have a cake board or plate ready. Add a dollop of chocolate ganache frosting to the center to adhere the first layer. Place the first cooled layer flat side down on the cake board. Trim the cake layer to level it. Add a generous amount of chocolate ganache frosting to the center and spread to the edges using a small offset spatula. Remove the next cake layer and trim with a serrated knife to level. Place on top of the first layer and frost with chocolate ganache. For the last cake layer, trim it to level, then place cut side down, so you have a flat and level top of the cake. Frost the entire exterior of the cake with the chocolate ganache. Refrigerate for 15 minutes. Remove cake from fridge and frost with a second final layer of chocolate ganache. Using a fork, create scraggly drags through the chocolate to mimic fur.

Using the black fondant, create thick triangles for the ears. Insert wooden skewers into the ears to anchor them to the cake.

Using the yellow fondant, cut out large almond-shaped eyes using a paring knife. Add black irises, if desired. Add a pink nose, and a black fondant mouth and whiskers. Add yellow or white sharp teeth, if desired.

Two-Faced Mayor Red Velvet Cake

Halloween Town's Mayor is a frightfully two-faced character—when he's happy, we see his gleeful smile, but when he's upset, his head rotates to show his dismay on a pale face with a toothy frown. Inspired by the multifaceted Mayor, this red velvet cake displays wonderfully on a cake turntable to swap between his two moods just as quickly as the Mayor himself. But there will be no sour faces as you enjoy this delicious treat!

Yield: 1 cake, 18 to 20 servings | Skill Level: Moderate

FOR THE RED VELVET CAKE

3 large eggs, room temperature
¾ cup vegetable oil
1¾ cups buttermilk, room temperature
1 tablespoon white vinegar
¾ cup unsalted butter, melted and cooled
2 teaspoons pure vanilla extract
2 tablespoons red gel food coloring
3½ cups all-purpose flour
2½ cups granulated sugar
¼ cup Dutch-process cocoa powder
1½ teaspoons fine sea salt
2 teaspoons baking soda

FOR THE CREAM CHEESE FROSTING

1 cup cream cheese, room temperature
1 cup unsalted butter, room temperature
4 cups icing sugar
2 teaspoons pure vanilla extract
Pinch of salt

DECORATING INGREDIENTS AND TOOLS

8-by-2-inch round cake pan
7-by-2-inch round cake pan
6-by-3-inch round cake pan
Serrated knife
Cake board or cake plate
Cake bench scraper
Peach-colored gel food coloring
Black, white, yellow, and pink or red fondant
Chopstick or toothpick
Small offset spatula
Wooden skewer, cut in half

TO MAKE THE CAKES: Preheat oven to 350°F.

Spray each baking pan generously with nonstick cooking spray, line each with parchment paper cut to size, and spray again. Set aside.

In a large bowl, mix together the eggs, vegetable oil, buttermilk, vinegar, melted butter, vanilla, and red gel food coloring and set aside.

In the bowl of a stand mixer fitted with the paddle attachment or a large bowl with a handheld mixer, mix together on low speed the flour, sugar, cocoa powder, salt, and baking soda to combine.

With the mixer on low speed, carefully add the oil mixture to the flour mixture, mixing until incorporated and a smooth batter forms, scraping down the sides of the bowl as needed, about 1 minute total.

Divide the cake batter into the cake pans: Fill each ⅔ full, with a little more in the 6-by-3-inch round cake pan. Bake at varying times—the 8-inch cake takes about 22 minutes, the 7-inch cake about 20 minutes, and the 6-inch cake about 18 minutes—until the cakes are baked through, the top springs back to the touch, and a toothpick inserted into the center comes out with only moist crumbs.

Let cool completely in the pans on wire racks.

TO MAKE THE FROSTING: In the bowl of a stand mixer fitted with the paddle attachment or a large bowl with a handheld mixer, beat the cream cheese, butter, icing sugar, vanilla extract, and salt on low speed to combine. Increase to medium speed and beat until thick and creamy, about 2 minutes.

CONTINUES ON PAGE 116

TO ASSEMBLE THE CAKE: Turn the cakes out of their cake pans and trim and level the cakes using a serrated knife.

Place a dollop of cream cheese frosting on a cake board or cake plate and place the 8-inch cake on the platter, pressing into the cream cheese frosting to adhere. Frost a generous amount of cream cheese frosting on top, then top with the 7-inch cake, frost the top, then add the taller 6-inch cake. Refrigerate for 15 minutes to firm up. Using a sharp serrated knife, trim the stacked cakes into a thick cone-like shape.

Frost the entire cake with the frosting, using a cake bench scraper to smooth. Refrigerate for 20 minutes, until firm.

Divide the remaining frosting—place ½ cup into a small bowl, tinting with ¼ teaspoon of peach gel food coloring to make a "skin" tone.

MAKE ALL THE FONDANT FACIAL FEATURES FOR HAPPY MAYOR AND SAD MAYOR:

Happy Face:
- 1 black fondant eye
- 1 black fondant swirl eye
- Black movement lines for around the eyes
- Black fondant nose
- Red or pink fondant mouth
- Red or pink dots for cheeks
- White teeth with black teeth lines
- White iris

Sad Face:
- Round yellow eyes
- Black dots for irises
- Black nose
- Black mouth with white sharp teeth
- Black lines for movement lines

Remove the cake from the refrigerator. Using a chopstick or toothpick, differentiate a line on the side of the cake, working your way up and around, to delineate Happy Mayor and Sad Mayor. For the Happy Mayor, carefully add a layer of peachy skin-colored frosting. Smooth with a small offset spatula.

Place the facial features on both sides of the Mayor's face. To make the black top hat, punch out a 2-inch round thick black disk or mold one with your hands for the top hat base. Roll together a thick, wonky column for the top hat "top," skewering it with the wooden skewer to anchor it to the cake. Pierce the top hat base and anchor the hat to the top of the cake. Add a band of white fondant to the top hat, using a tiny amount of water to adhere to the hat.

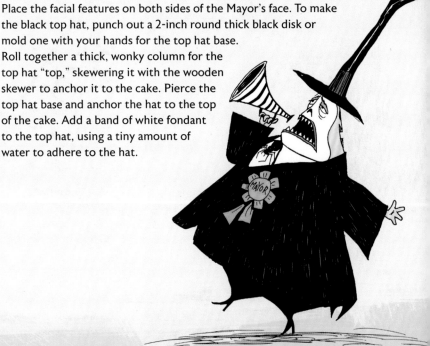

Tiny Head Sandy Claws Gingerbread Christmas Cake

Plump and kindhearted Sandy Claws is plucked from his snowy Christmas Town and plopped right into the wild, chaotic, and creepily charming world of Halloween Town! Your guests will get a kick out of this Jolly Old Saint Nick in corpulent cake form with a tiny cake-pop head!

Yield: 1 cake, 12 to 16 servings | Skill Level: Advanced

FOR THE LEMON GINGERBREAD CAKES

3 large eggs, room temperature
²⁄₃ cup molasses
1 tablespoon lemon zest
2 teaspoons pure vanilla extract
2 cups cake flour
1 tablespoon baking powder
1 teaspoon fine sea salt
2 teaspoons ground cinnamon
2 teaspoons ground ginger
1 teaspoon ground nutmeg
1⅓ cups dark brown sugar
⅓ cup unsalted butter, room temperature
⅓ cup vegetable oil
¾ cup buttermilk

FOR THE VANILLA BUTTERCREAM

1½ cups unsalted butter, room temperature
3 cups icing sugar
2 teaspoons pure vanilla extract
Pinch of salt

FOR THE GINGER SPICE BUTTERCREAM

1 cup unsalted butter, room temperature
2 cups icing sugar
½ teaspoon ground ginger
½ teaspoon ground cinnamon
3 tablespoons molasses
1 teaspoon pure vanilla extract
Pinch of salt

DECORATING INGREDIENTS AND TOOLS

Two 6-by-3-inch round cake pans
6-inch-diameter sports-ball pan
Serrated knife
Cake board or cake platter
Wooden skewer or bubble tea straw
Peach-colored gel food coloring
Red gel food coloring
Black fondant
Wooden skewer, cut in half
Piping bag fitted with a small open circle tip
Piping bag fitted with a multi-opening tip (grass tip)
Piping bag fitted with a medium open circle tip
Offset spatula
White fondant

TO MAKE THE CAKES: Preheat the oven to 350°F. Spray each cake pan with nonstick cooking spray. Line the flat cake pans with parchment paper cut to size. Set aside.

In a medium bowl, whisk the eggs, molasses, lemon zest, and vanilla extract together until smooth.

In the bowl of a stand mixer fitted with the paddle attachment or a large bowl with a handheld mixer, mix together on low speed the flour, baking powder, salt, cinnamon, ginger, and nutmeg. Add the brown sugar and mix to incorporate. With the mixer on low speed, add the butter and the vegetable oil until the mixture resembles a coarse meal. With the mixer on low speed, slowly pour in the egg mixture until incorporated, then slowly pour in the buttermilk, scraping down the sides of the bowl as needed, until a smooth batter forms, 30 to 60 seconds.

Fill the sports-ball pan 2/3 full, then divide the remaining batter between the two 6-inch cake pans. Note: The rounded sports-ball pan will take much longer to bake. Bake for 18 to 22 minutes, until lightly browned and fragrant and a toothpick inserted into the center comes out with only moist crumbs. Continue baking the rounded sports-ball pan for another 15 to 20 minutes, or longer if necessary.

Let cakes cool completely on wire racks.

CONTINUES ON PAGE 120

TO MAKE THE VANILLA BUTTERCREAM: In the bowl of a stand mixer fitted with the paddle attachment or a large bowl with a handheld mixer, beat the butter, icing sugar, vanilla extract, and salt on low speed to combine. Increase to high speed and beat until light, fluffy, and doubled in volume, about 2 minutes.

TO MAKE THE GINGER SPICE BUTTERCREAM: In the bowl of a stand mixer fitted with the paddle attachment or a large bowl with a handheld mixer, beat the butter, icing sugar, ginger, cinnamon, molasses, vanilla extract, and salt on low speed to combine. Increase to high speed and beat until light, fluffy, and doubled in volume, about 2 minutes.

TO ASSEMBLE THE CAKE: Trim the cooled cakes with a serrated knife to level them. If a slight dome has baked onto the flat side of the sports-ball cake, trim the cake to level it. Reserve the cake scraps in a small bowl. Combine the cake scraps with ¼ cup ginger spice buttercream and mix to incorporate (you can add more of the buttercream as needed). The mixture should hold together in shape.

Using the mixture of scraps and buttercream, create a round cake-pop head shape for Sandy Claws's head. Freeze until firm, about 15 minutes.

Meanwhile, frost and fill the main body cake using the ginger spice buttercream. Place the first 6-inch cake layer on a cake board or cake platter. Fill generously with buttercream and place the second 6-inch layer on top. Fill generously with ginger spice buttercream. Place the rounded cake dome on top. Insert half a wooden skewer or bubble tea straw through the top center of the cakes to anchor them, if needed. Trim the skewer to size.

Divide the vanilla buttercream. Reserve 1 cup in a bowl for Sandy Claws's hair, long beard, and hat trim. Reserve ¼ cup for Sandy Claws's skin color and nose dot; color this with the peach gel.

Color the rest of the vanilla buttercream with 1 to 2 teaspoons of red gel color. Frost the entire exterior of the body cake with red buttercream and refrigerate until firm, about 20 minutes. Frost a second smooth coat of red buttercream, reserving some buttercream.

Remove the cake pop from the refrigerator. Frost it with the peach-colored buttercream. Freeze until firm, about 15 minutes.

Make a black belt out of black fondant. Make tiny little gloved hands. Set aside.

Remove the cake ball head from the freezer and insert half a wooden skewer into the bottom, anchoring the head into the top of the body by inserting the wooden skewer into the cake.

Using the white buttercream, fill two piping bags, one with a small open circle tip, and one with the multi-opening tip. Use the multi-opening tip to pipe hair onto Sandy's head. Pipe hair and a continuous thick long beard all the way down Sandy's body. If you mess up, carefully remove the hair with an offset spatula and pipe it again on top!

Fill the piping bag fitted with the medium open circle tip with the reserved red buttercream. Pipe a hat on top of Sandy's head by squeezing the piping bag at a 90 degree angle, then pulling upward to release. Place a small white fondant ball on top of the hat. Pipe Sandy's arms along the side of the cake. Place a little black glove at the end of each arm. Use the piping bag fitted with the small open circle tip filled with white buttercream to pipe trimming along Sandy's hat edge and mitt cuffs.

Using the white and black fondant, make little eyeballs and irises for Sandy, pressing into the cake ball head to adhere, using a tiny amount of water. Make a little black mouth for Sandy and press into the buttercream to adhere. Using the peach buttercream, carefully add a little blob onto Sandy's face for his nose.

Halloween Yule Log Chocolate Orange Cake

Yule log? More like *ghoul* log! This Halloween take on a classic Christmas tradition features chocolate orange flavors and "mushrooms" perched atop a delightful chocolate ganache log. Inspired by the magical Holiday Doors that Jack discovers in the forest, this yule log features a striated bark-like texture created using the prongs of a fork! Note: The meringue mushrooms should be prepared one day ahead of serving.

Yield: 1 cake, 10 to 12 servings | Skill Level: Moderate

FOR THE SWISS MERINGUE MUSHROOMS

½ lemon

½ cup egg whites (about 4 large egg whites)

1 cup granulated sugar

1 teaspoon pure vanilla extract

FOR THE CHOCOLATE ORANGE ROLL CAKE

½ cup all-purpose flour

⅓ cup Dutch-process cocoa powder, plus more for dusting

2 teaspoons instant espresso powder

1 teaspoon baking powder

½ teaspoon fine sea salt

5 large eggs, room temperature

1 cup granulated sugar

3 tablespoons vegetable oil

1 teaspoon pure orange extract

FOR THE CHOCOLATE ORANGE GANACHE

1 cup heavy cream

2 cups best-quality dark or bittersweet chocolate

1 teaspoon orange liqueur or pure orange extract

FOR THE ORANGE ZEST WHIPPED CREAM

1½ cups heavy cream

1 tablespoon fresh orange juice

½ cup icing sugar, plus more for dusting

1 tablespoon finely grated orange zest

DECORATING INGREDIENTS AND TOOLS

Orange gel food coloring

2 large baking sheets

2 piping bags fitted with large open circle tips

13-by-18-inch rimmed baking sheet or jelly roll pan

Rubber spatula (optional)

Offset spatula

Cake board or cake platter

Knife

Large, clean tea towel

Japanese chocolate mushroom cookies (optional, if not making meringue mushrooms)

Rosemary sprigs (optional)

Candy bugs (optional)

Mini candy canes or peppermint swirl candies (optional)

Candy thermometer

TO MAKE THE MERINGUE MUSHROOMS: Ensure that the metal bowl of your stand mixer is completely grease-free by wiping it with a halved lemon, then rinse and dry it thoroughly.

In the bowl of a stand mixer fitted with the whisk attachment or a large bowl with a handheld mixer, mix the egg whites and sugar on low speed to combine into a sugar slurry. Fill a medium saucepan with a few inches of water and place it on the stove over medium-high heat. Set the mixer bowl on top of the saucepan to create a double boiler, making sure the mixer bowl doesn't touch the water.

Heat the egg and sugar mixture until it reaches 160°F on a thermometer, whisking occasionally, 5 to 7 minutes.

Carefully return the mixing bowl to the stand mixer, with the whisk attachment in place. Bring the mixer up to high speed and beat the mixture for 8 to 10 minutes, until you've reached stiff peaks, a billowy meringue. Add the vanilla extract and whip on high speed to combine, about 15 seconds.

CONTINUES ON PAGE 124

Divide the meringue; place 1 cup in a separate bowl and carefully fold in ½ teaspoon of orange gel food coloring.

Preheat the oven to 200°F.

Line two large baking sheets with parchment paper. Fill a piping bag fitted with a large open circle tip with the orange meringue. Pipe dollops of orange meringue on the prepared baking sheet, using a clean finger dampened with a bit of water to press down the meringue into a mushroom cap shape. Fill the second piping bag fitted with a large open circle tip with the white meringue. Pipe stems for the mushrooms, pressing down with a damp finger if needed.

Bake until crisp, 1 to 1½ hours, being careful they don't brown. Turn the oven off completely and allow the meringue mushrooms to dry out overnight.

TO MAKE THE CAKE: Preheat the oven to 350°F. Spray a 13-by-18-inch rimmed baking sheet or jelly roll pan with nonstick cooking spray and line with parchment paper cut to size. Spray the parchment paper. Set aside.

In a medium bowl, whisk together the flour, cocoa powder, espresso powder, baking powder, and salt.

In the bowl of a stand mixer fitted with the paddle attachment or a large bowl with a handheld mixer, beat the eggs on medium speed until light and foamy, about 3 minutes. Increase to high speed, gradually adding in the sugar, beating until the eggs have lightened and volumized considerably, 4 to 5 minutes.

Reduce the speed to medium. Pour in the vegetable oil and orange extract, mixing to combine.

Turn the mixer off and add the flour mixture to the egg mixture. Mix on low speed to combine, until just incorporated, 15 to 20 seconds. Use a rubber spatula to carefully fold the rest of the batter together, if needed.

Pour the batter onto the prepared baking sheet, using an offset spatula to spread to the edges. Bake for 12 to 14 minutes, being careful not to overbake, or until a toothpick inserted into the center of the cake comes out with only moist crumbs.

While the cake is in the oven, prepare a clean work surface: Place a clean tea towel on the counter with the longer side closest to you and dust lightly with cocoa powder.

Remove the cake from the oven and immediately and carefully run an offset spatula around the edges of the pan to help release the cake. Lightly dust the top with cocoa powder, and invert onto the prepared kitchen towel. Carefully peel off the parchment paper and lightly dust with more cocoa powder.

Now it's time to roll up the cake. Carefully start to roll the short side of the cake, along with the tea towel, into a tight roll. Place the rolled-up cake seam side down on a wire rack and let cool completely to room temperature.

TO MAKE THE GANACHE: In a medium saucepan over medium heat, bring the cream to a low boil. Remove the pan from the heat and add the chocolate, swirling the pan so the cream covers the chocolate entirely. Let sit for 10 minutes. Add the orange liqueur, then whisk carefully together until smooth and glossy. Allow to cool to a frosting spreadability. The ganache will thicken as it cools; refrigerate it to speed up the process, about 30 minutes, being careful not to solidify it.

TO MAKE THE WHIPPED CREAM: In the bowl of a stand mixer fitted with the whisk attachment or a large bowl with a handheld mixer, whip the cream on high speed until medium peaks form, about 2 minutes. Add the orange juice and whip until thickened, about 2 more minutes. Add the icing sugar, orange zest, and ¼ teaspoon orange gel color and whip until stiff peaks form, about 2 more minutes, being careful not to overwhip!

TO ASSEMBLE THE CAKE: Very carefully unroll the cooled cake. Using an offset spatula, spread the orange whipped cream onto the cake in an even layer, leaving a ¼-inch border so the whipped cream doesn't ooze out. Gently reroll the cake (without the tea towel!). (Don't fret if you have cracks in the cake—it will be covered completely with delicious chocolate ganache.)

Prepare your cake board or cake platter. Place the log onto the cake board. Assemble meringue mushrooms by using a small dollop of chocolate ganache to attach the mushroom stems to the tops.

Trim at an angle a 3-inch piece off the roll cake. Arrange the cut piece against the roll. Carefully frost the exterior of the cake, leaving the cut edges visible. Using a fork, drag the prongs through the log to create striations similar to bark. Dust the whole cake lightly with icing sugar and, if desired, adorn with the orange meringue mushrooms or mushroom cookies, rosemary sprigs, candy bugs, and candy cane–themed candies.

Vampire Teddy Black Forest Cake

Beary Christmas! Dessert is served! Dark chocolate layers, cherry syrup, and preserved sour cherries will make your Vampire Teddy Black Forest Cake roar with deliciousness. If you can't find sour cherries, feel free to use maraschino cherries. Note: The black candy melt ears or chocolate ears can be made the day before.

Yield: 1 cake, 12 to 16 servings | Skill Level: Moderate

FOR THE CHOCOLATE CAKE

⅔ cup all-purpose flour
½ cup Dutch-process cocoa powder
½ teaspoon fine sea salt
6 large eggs, room temperature
1¼ cups granulated sugar
1 teaspoon pure vanilla extract
¾ cup unsalted butter, melted and cooled

FOR THE CHERRY SYRUP

2 cups pitted morello cherries (sour cherries) in syrup
¾ cup reserved cherry juice
½ cup granulated sugar

FOR THE VANILLA BUTTERCREAM

2 cups unsalted butter, room temperature
4 cups icing sugar
1 teaspoon pure vanilla extract
Pinch of salt

FOR THE BLACK COCOA POWDER BUTTERCREAM

1 cup unsalted butter, room temperature
2 cups icing sugar
¼ cup black cocoa powder
¼ cup Dutch-process cocoa powder
2 teaspoons pure vanilla extract
2 tablespoons whole milk, room temperature
¼ teaspoon fine sea salt
1 teaspoon super black gel color

DECORATING INGREDIENTS AND TOOLS

Three 7-by-2-inch round cake pans
Rubber spatula
One 12-ounce package black candy melts
Set of 2-inch round cookie or chocolate lollipop molds
Lollipop sticks
Round cake board or cake platter
Red gel food coloring
Cake bench scraper
Wooden skewer or chopstick
2 piping bags fitted with small open circle tips
Small offset spatula
White fondant
Black fondant (optional)
2 plain round large circle chocolate lollipops (optional)

TO MAKE THE CAKE: Preheat oven to 350°F. Spray the cake pans with nonstick cooking spray, and line each with parchment paper cut to size. Spray again and set aside.

In a medium bowl, whisk together the flour, cocoa powder, and salt and set aside.

In the bowl of a stand mixer fitted with the whisk attachment or a large bowl with a handheld mixer, whisk the eggs on medium speed for 30 seconds. Slowly add the sugar with the mixer on low speed. Add the vanilla extract.

Increase to high speed and beat the egg and sugar mixture until tripled in volume and pale in color.

With the mixer turned off, add the flour mixture. Use a rubber spatula to carefully fold in the flour mixture, being conscious not to deflate the egg mixture. Carefully fold in the melted and cooled butter.

Divide the batter evenly between the prepared cake pans and bake for 22 to 25 minutes, until the cakes are springy to the touch and a toothpick inserted into the center of the cake comes out with only moist crumbs.

Cool completely on wire racks.

CONTINUES ON PAGE 128

TO MAKE THE CHERRY SYRUP: Using a fine mesh strainer, drain the jar of morello cherries, reserving the cherry juice.

In a small saucepan, heat over medium heat the ¾ cup of cherry juice with the granulated sugar until the sugar dissolves, reducing to thicken into a syrup, about 2 minutes. Let cool completely before using.

TO MAKE THE VANILLA BUTTERCREAM: In the bowl of a stand mixer fitted with the paddle attachment or a large bowl with a handheld mixer, beat the butter, icing sugar, vanilla extract, and salt on low speed to combine. Increase to high speed and beat until light, fluffy, and doubled in volume, about 2 minutes.

TO MAKE THE BLACK COCOA BUTTERCREAM: In the bowl of a stand mixer fitted with the paddle attachment or a large bowl with a handheld mixer, beat the butter, icing sugar, black cocoa powder, Dutch-process cocoa powder, vanilla extract, whole milk, salt, and black gel color on low speed to combine. Increase to high speed and beat until fluffy and doubled in volume, about 2 minutes. Note: The buttercream will darken further as it sits.

TO ASSEMBLE THE CAKE: Make the ears: Prepare the black candy melts and pour them into the lollipop molds, adding the lollipop sticks. Allow to cool and harden completely.

Prepare a round cake board or cake platter.

Reserve ¼ cup vanilla buttercream to a small bowl; tint with ½ teaspoon red gel color.

Add a dollop of white vanilla buttercream to the cake board and then place the first chocolate cake layer on top, trimming to level if needed. Add a generous amount of cherry syrup to the first layer, then frost with vanilla buttercream. Place drained morello cherries directly and deeply into the buttercream, nestling them in an even pattern. Place the next cake layer on top, pressing down to adhere. Repeat the cherry syrup, vanilla buttercream, and cherries. Top with the final layer; add more syrup to the top layer, then frost the entire cake with a thin layer of vanilla buttercream. Refrigerate for 20 minutes to firm up. Remove from fridge and frost again, smoothing the cake with a cake bench scraper.

Using a wooden skewer or chopstick, draw the widow's peak of the Vampire Teddy in the frosting. Fill a piping bag fitted with a small open circle tip with black buttercream. Pipe the outline of the widow's peak and the outline border of the entire top of the cake. Using a small offset spatula, frost the inside of the outline using the black buttercream, smoothing with spatula.

Cut out the white fondant eyes and sharp teeth, and black fondant eye irises and nose and set aside. Attach the black irises to the white eyes with a tiny amount of water to adhere. Place the eyes and nose onto the cake. Alternatively, cut out 2 thick black fondant circles, attach to lollipop sticks by inserting the sticks into the fondant, and dry overnight, or 2 plain round large circle chocolate lollipops for the eyes. Fill the second piping bag fitted with the small open circle tip with the red buttercream. Pipe a creepy smile onto the cake. Add the white teeth. Place the black ears into the top of the cake.

Creepy Christmas Gift Box Eggnog Cake

Forget cuddly teddy bears, train sets, and dollies . . . how about a friendly, lovable, tantalizingly tentacled monster? Jack Skellington has good intentions, but he and the citizens of Halloween Town can't help but add some good-natured fright to Christmas morning's gift-giving festivities!

Yield: 1 cake, 12 to 16 servings | Skill Level: Advanced

FOR THE EGGNOG CAKE

- ½ cup unsalted butter, room temperature
- 1¼ cups granulated sugar
- 3 large eggs, room temperature
- 1 teaspoon pure vanilla extract
- 1 teaspoon rum extract
- 2 cups all-purpose flour
- 2 teaspoons baking powder
- 1 teaspoon fine sea salt
- 1 cup full-fat eggnog, plus ½ cup additional for eggnog cake soak

FOR THE EGGNOG BUTTERCREAM

- 2 cups unsalted butter, room temperature
- 4 cups icing sugar
- 1 teaspoon rum extract
- 1 teaspoon pure vanilla extract
- 2 tablespoons eggnog (or more, if desired)
- Pinch of salt
- Green gel food coloring

DECORATING INGREDIENTS AND TOOLS

- Two 6-by-2-inch square cake pans
- Cake board or cake platter
- Serrated knife
- Cake bench scraper
- 24 prepackaged puffed rice cereal treats (or make your own)
- Wooden skewers
- Piping bag fitted with a leaf tip
- Red fondant
- White fondant

TO MAKE THE CAKE: Preheat the oven to 350°F. Spray cake pans with nonstick cooking spray and line with parchment paper circles cut to size. Spray again and set aside.

In the bowl of a stand mixer fitted with the paddle attachment or a large bowl with a handheld mixer, beat together on high speed the butter and sugar until light, fluffy, and doubled in volume, about 2 minutes, scraping down the sides of the bowl as needed. With the mixer on low speed, add the eggs, one at a time, beating to combine after each addition. Add the vanilla extract and rum extract and mix to incorporate.

In a medium bowl, whisk together the flour, baking powder, and salt.

Add the flour mixture to the butter mixture in three additions, alternating with the eggnog and beginning and ending with the flour mixture, until a smooth batter forms, 30 to 60 seconds.

Divide the batter evenly between the two cake pans and bake for 30 to 32 minutes, until lightly browned and a toothpick inserted into the center of the cake comes out with only moist crumbs. Let cool completely on wire racks.

TO MAKE THE BUTTERCREAM: In the bowl of a stand mixer fitted with the paddle attachment or a large bowl with a handheld mixer, beat the butter, icing sugar, rum extract, vanilla extract, eggnog to taste, and salt on low speed to combine. Increase to high speed and beat until light, fluffy, and doubled in volume, about 2 minutes. Place 1 cup of buttercream into a small bowl and tint using the gel food coloring.

TO ASSEMBLE THE CAKE: Prepare a cake board or cake platter. Remove the cakes from their pans and trim and level them using a serrated knife, then cut them in half horizontally to make four layers. Fill and frost the cake: Place the first cake layer onto your cake board or plate, using a dollop of white buttercream to adhere. Using a pastry brush or teaspoon, add a generous amount of eggnog to soak the cake layer. Add a layer of white buttercream, then place the next layer on top, repeating the eggnog cake soak with all layers. Frost the entire exterior of the cake, smoothing with a cake bench scraper. Refrigerate until firm, about 20 minutes. Remove the cake and carve out two large holes at the upper corners of the front of the cake.

CONTINUES ON PAGE 131

Mold the puffed rice cereal treats into tentacles that will fit into the holes you cut out. Lay the end tips of the tentacles to sit on the cake board to help hold any excess weight. Once you've figured out how to insert the tentacles, prepare a small piece of parchment paper on a plate. Frost the puffed rice cereal treat tentacle shapes with green buttercream. Freeze the tentacles for 20 minutes to set. Remove from freezer, then insert into the holes of the cake and against the cake using wooden skewers cut to size, as needed. Fill the piping bag fitted with the leaf tip with the remaining green buttercream. Adorn the tentacles by piping scale-like shapes onto the tentacles.

Meanwhile, prepare the fondant ribbon. Cut out thick strips of red fondant to adorn the cake as if it's wrapped with a tight ribbon. To create the giant bow, roll out a ¼-inch-thick layer of fondant in a long wide rectangle shape, 12 inches long. Cut into two 6-inch pieces. Using a balled-up piece of paper towel, fold over the edge of one 6-inch piece of fondant using the paper towel to keep its shape, and adhere the two edges together using a tiny amount of water as glue. You will have one side of the bow made, resting on the paper towel to hold the bow shape. Pinch the edges together to form a ripple. Repeat with the second side of the bow, matching the two pieces and pinching them together to combine. Create the center of the bow by cutting a smaller rectangular shape to wrap around the center, sealing it in the back of the bow. The bow should be able to stand upright. Create two "trimmed ribbon" pieces using fondant to tuck under the bow and hang over the cake.

Punch out white fondant circles for tentacle suckers and press into the green buttercream tentacles. Place the ribbon trimmings on the top of the cake. Place the giant bow on top of the ribbon trimmings, anchoring with a wooden skewer, if needed.

Zero the Dog Peppermint Half Cake

Man's best friend, whether you're dead or alive, is a dog. And for Jack Skellington, his best friend is Zero the dog! This cake, inspired by Zero, is in cute *kawaii* half-cake form! Once you've made this cake, you can use the other half-cake to make an accompanying Jack Skellington cake! This version uses mint chocolate sandwich cookies chopped up into minty buttercream and dark chocolate cake layers to be as cool as Zero's core temperature.

Yield: 1 cake, 10 to 12 servings | Skill Level: Moderate

FOR THE CHOCOLATE CAKE

2½ cups all-purpose flour
1¼ cups Dutch-process cocoa powder
2 cups granulated sugar
2 teaspoons baking soda
1 teaspoon baking powder
1 teaspoon fine sea salt
2 large eggs
1¼ cups whole milk
½ cup vegetable oil
2 teaspoons pure vanilla extract
1 cup hot coffee

FOR THE PEPPERMINT BUTTERCREAM

2 cups unsalted butter, room temperature
4 cups icing sugar
1 teaspoon pure peppermint extract
Pinch of salt

DECORATING INGREDIENTS AND TOOLS

Three 7-by-2-inch round cake pans
1 package mint chocolate sandwich cookies
Resealable plastic bag
Serrated knife
2 cake boards or cake platters
Large sharp knife
White fondant
2 wooden skewers
Tiny pumpkin candy such as a Mellowcreme, or orange fondant or orange candy
Black fondant

TO MAKE THE CAKE: Preheat the oven to 350°F. Spray the cake pans with nonstick cooking spray, then line with parchment paper circles cut to size. Spray the parchment paper and set aside.

In the bowl of a stand mixer fitted with the paddle attachment or a large bowl with a handheld mixer, combine on low speed the flour, cocoa powder, sugar, baking soda, baking powder, and salt.

Add the eggs, milk, vegetable oil, vanilla, and coffee. Beat on low speed until combined and smooth, about 2 minutes, scraping down the sides of the bowl as needed.

Divide the batter evenly among the 3 prepared cake pans and bake for 22 to 25 minutes, until the tops of the cakes are springy and a toothpick inserted into the center of the cake comes out with only moist crumbs. Let cool completely.

TO MAKE THE BUTTERCREAM: In the bowl of a stand mixer fitted with the paddle attachment or a large bowl with a handheld mixer, beat the butter, icing sugar, peppermint extract, and salt on low speed to combine. Increase to high speed and beat until light, fluffy, and doubled in volume, about 2 minutes.

TO ASSEMBLE THE CAKE: Place 20 mint chocolate sandwich cookies in a resealable plastic bag. Using a rolling pin, crush the cookies into small pieces.

Remove the cake layers from their pans, using a serrated knife to trim and level them. Place a dollop of buttercream on a cake board or cake platter; place the first layer on top. Top with a generous amount of buttercream, then add crushed cookie pieces and nestle them right into the buttercream. Cover with the next cake layer and repeat, then top with the final cake layer. Frost the entire cake with buttercream, then refrigerate for 20 minutes to set. Frost a final smooth cake layer and refrigerate again for 20 minutes, until set.

Remove the cake from the refrigerator. Using a large sharp knife, cut the cake in half vertically through the center, placing one half-cake cut-side down on a different cake board. Position the half-cake on the current cake board so that it's cut-side down. Frost the exposed side of both sides with the peppermint buttercream. If needed, clean up the cake boards with a paper towel to remove any excess chocolate cake crumbs or buttercream.

Using the white fondant, make two thick, long ear-like pieces about three inches long. Insert a wooden skewer into each. Insert them into the top back of the cake for Zero's ears.

Mold a cone-like shape out of white fondant, turning the point of the cone upward. Press the fondant cone up against the cake for Zero's long nose. Add a dot of buttercream to the tip of the nose and stick the Mellowcreme pumpkin or orange candy on top.

Using the black fondant, make 1-inch round eyes for Zero by rolling the fondant into two balls. Add two tiny white fondant eye highlights, adhering them with a tiny amount of water. Press the eyes into the buttercream to adhere.

Creepy Candy Bug Cake

Well, well, well—what have we here?! A creepy Oogie Boogie surprise inside, so you might recoil in fear! This neon green Oogie Boogie 3D cake will split at the seams, revealing a body made up of icky bugs, petrifying critters, and slimy insects—just like Oogie Boogie himself!

Yield: 1 cake, 10 to 12 servings | Skill Level: Advanced

FOR THE FUNFETTI CAKE

3 cups cake flour

1 tablespoon baking powder

½ teaspoon baking soda

1 teaspoon fine sea salt

1 cup unsalted butter, room temperature

2 cups granulated sugar

4 eggs

2 teaspoons pure vanilla extract

1½ cups buttermilk

1 cup rainbow sprinkles (not naturally colored)

FOR THE VANILLA BUTTERCREAM

2 cups unsalted butter

4 cups icing sugar

2 teaspoons pure vanilla extract

Pinch of salt

DECORATING INGREDIENTS AND TOOLS

8-by-2-inch round cake pan

7-by-2-inch round cake pan

6-by-2-inch round cake pan

6-inch-diameter sports-ball pan

Neon green gel food coloring

Cake board or cake platter

Serrated knife

Circle cookie cutter

Gummy worms

Candy bugs

Sharp knife

Offset spatula or fork

Black fondant

TO MAKE THE CAKE: Preheat the oven to 350°F. Spray each cake pan with nonstick cooking spray. Line the flat cake pans with parchment paper cut to size. Set aside.

In a large bowl, whisk to combine the flour, baking powder, baking soda, and salt.

In the bowl of a stand mixer fitted with the paddle attachment or a large bowl with a hand mixer, beat the butter and sugar on high speed until light, fluffy, and doubled in volume, about 2 minutes, scraping down the sides of the bowl as needed. Add the eggs on low speed, one at a time, until incorporated. Add the vanilla extract and mix on low speed to combine, about fifteen seconds.

With the mixer on low speed, add the flour mixture to the butter mixture in three additions, alternating with the buttermilk, beginning and ending with the flour mixture, until a smooth batter forms, 30 to 60 seconds. Carefully fold in the rainbow sprinkles in two or three turns, being careful not to overmix.

Divide the batter evenly among the prepared cake pans, filling about ⅔ full.

Bake the cakes. Note that the cakes will have different baking times depending on pan size. Bake the round cakes for 22 to 24 minutes, until lightly golden and a toothpick inserted into the center comes out with only moist crumbs. Bake the ball-shaped cake for 30 to 35 minutes. Let cakes cool completely in their pans on wire racks.

TO MAKE THE BUTTERCREAM: In the bowl of a stand mixer fitted with the paddle attachment or a large bowl with a handheld mixer, beat the butter, icing sugar, vanilla extract, and salt on low speed to combine. Increase to high speed and beat until light, fluffy, and doubled in volume, about 2 minutes.

CONTINUES ON PAGE 136

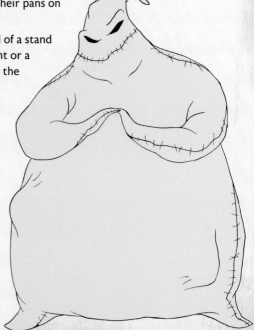

135

TO ASSEMBLE THE CAKE: Color the buttercream using 1 teaspoon of neon green gel color.

Prepare a cake board or cake platter. Trim and level the cake layers using a serrated knife, reserving the scraps. Using a circle cookie cutter, cut out a hole in the center of each of the three now flattened cake layers, reserving the cake cut-outs.

Place a dollop of the neon green buttercream on the cake board and place the 8-inch round cake layer on top. Frost the cake layer with the buttercream, without filling the cut-out hole. Stack the 7-inch cake layer on top and frost. Repeat with the 6-inch cake layer, with the center hole now going down the entire cake. Stuff gummy worms and candy bugs into the center hole; place one reserved round cake cut-out back into the top of the hole and level it by pressing down. Add buttercream frosting to this top layer, then add the ball-shaped 6-inch layer. Carefully carve the cake using a sharp knife to give it more of a fat cone-like shape (like Oogie Boogie's head).

Mix the remaining cake scraps with the green buttercream to create a cake-pop molding consistency, and mold the shape for Oogie Boogie's pointy sack at the top of his head. Refrigerate the pointy piece until firm, about 15 minutes. Use buttercream to adhere it to the top of the cake. Frost the entire exterior of the cake with the green buttercream, then refrigerate until firm, about 20 minutes.

Remove the cake from the refrigerator and apply a final coat of buttercream, using an offset spatula or a fork to create a burlap-like rustic pattern on Oogie Boogie. Using the black fondant, mold two teardrop-shaped eyes and a mouth in the shape of a crescent moon. Apply his eyes and mouth by pressing gently into the buttercream. Create a few "stitches" using black fondant and place them on Oogie Boogie's head. Strategically position a few bugs that got away on Oogie and on the cake board!

Acknowledgments

Thank you to Insight Editions and Anna Wostenberg for this fun opportunity. Thank you to Tim Burton for the incredible inspiration for the book's projects and recipes. Thank you always to my husband, Dr. Dixon Nutsworth; my son, T. Nutsworth; and our beloved feline friends, Potato Chip and Percival "Percy" the Fluffball. Thank you to my parents, the Snuglys, and my entire family.

With love, from

SANDY K. SNUGLY

Measurement Conversions

VOLUME

US	Metric
⅕ teaspoon (tsp)	1 ml
1 teaspoon (tsp)	5 ml
1 tablespoon (tbsp)	15 ml
1 fluid ounce (fl. oz.)	30 ml
⅕ cup	50 ml
¼ cup	60 ml
⅔ cup	80 ml
3.4 fluid ounces (fl. oz.)	100 ml
½ cup	120 ml
⅔ cup	160 ml
¾ cup	180 ml
1 cup	240 ml
1 pint (2 cups)	480 ml
1 quart (4 cups)	.95 liter

TEMPERATURES

Fahrenheit	Celsius
200°	93.3°
212°	100°
250°	120°
275°	135°
300°	150°
325°	163°
350°	177°
400°	205°
425°	218°
450°	232°
475°	246°

WEIGHT

US	Metric
0.5 ounce (oz.)	14 grams (g)
1 ounce (oz.)	28 grams (g)
¼ pound (lb.)	113 grams (g)
⅓ pound (lb.)	151 grams (g)
½ pound (lb.)	227 grams (g)
1 pound (lb.)	454 grams (g)

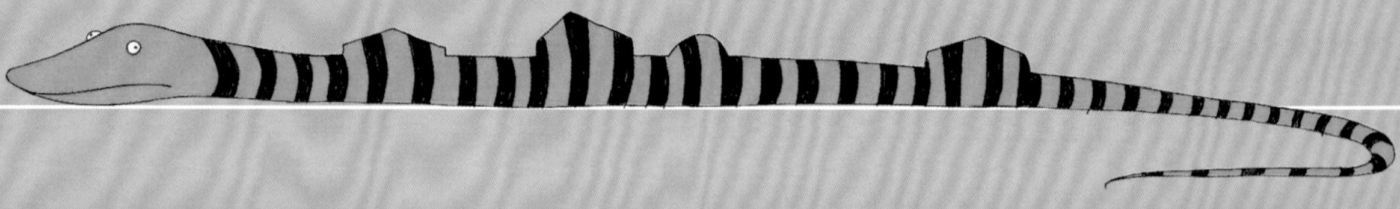

Notes

INSIGHT
EDITIONS

PO Box 3088
San Rafael, CA 94912
www.insighteditions.com

 Find us on Facebook: www.facebook.com/InsightEditions
 Follow us on Twitter: @insighteditions
 Follow us on Instagram: @insighteditions

ISBN: 979-8-88663-186-9
Gift ISBN: 979-8-88663-276-7

Publisher: Raoul Goff
VP, Co-Publisher: Vanessa Lopez
VP, Creative: Chrissy Kwasnik
VP, Manufacturing: Alix Nicholaeff
VP, Group Managing Editor: Vicki Jaeger
Publishing Director: Jamie Thompson
Senior Designer: Judy Wiatrek Trum
Editor: Anna Wostenberg
Editorial Assistant: Sami Alvarado
Managing Editor: Maria Spano
Senior Production Editor: Michael Hylton
Production Associate: Deena Hashem
Senior Production Manager, Subsidiary Rights: Lina s Palma-Temena

Photographer: Lorena Masso
Food Stylist: Victoria Woollard
Food Stylist: Amy Hatwig

Insight Editions, in association with Roots of Peace, will plant two trees for each tree used in the manufacturing of this book. Roots of Peace is an internationally renowned humanitarian organization dedicated to eradicating land mines worldwide and converting war-torn lands into productive farms and wildlife habitats. Roots of Peace will plant two million fruit and nut trees in Afghanistan and provide farmers there with the skills and support necessary for sustainable land use.

Manufactured in China by Insight Editions

10 9 8 7 6 5 4 3